The Whole Word Catalogue

edited by
Rosellen Brown
Marvin Hoffman
Martin Kushner
Phillip Lopate
Sheila Murphy

VIRGIL BOOKS

Virgil books are published by Teachers and Writers Collaborative
186 West 4th Street New York, N.Y. 10014

We are grateful to the publishers of the following
books for permission to reprint passages which appear
in this publication:

"Fun and Games with the English Language" by
Tony Kallet, *Outlook* (Issue 2, Spring 1971),
Mountain View Center for Environmental Education,
Univ. of Colo., Boulder, Colorado 80302.

Wishes, Lies and Dreams by Kenneth Koch, c. 1970,
Random House, Inc.

How to Survive in Your Native Land by James
Herndon, c.1971, Simon and Schuster.

The Essential Lenny Bruce compiled and edited by
John Cohen, c.1967. By permission of Douglas Book
Corporation.

Cover design by Adalberto Ortiz

Contents

BOOKS AND OTHER RESOURCES

Introduction

Teachers & Writers Collaborative was started in 1967 with the premise that professional writers and poets, given classrooms to teach, would find new approaches to making writing come alive for the students.

During the past four and a half years, TWC has worked mostly with students who were writing with great difficulty, either with no confidence, little personal success, or rarely with any pleasure. Many of the "forms" suggested here are starters—ice-breakers and pain relievers—towards a deeper involvement and greater enjoyment in writing. They have no sequence and cannot be used effectively as a writing curriculum.

We hope these are useful ideas. Some were created spontaneously by teachers in order to rescue an assignment which wasn't working or to recover from one of those familiar moments in class of total confusion. Frankly, much of what we here call "exercises" were accidents, strokes of luck conceived in the heat of teaching. They may never work as well again as they did in their conception. Other forms here suggested have withstood several classrooms; again and again, they have had rich and varied results.

Many of these ideas were developed in large classrooms of thirty kids in New York City public schools. Nevertheless, they can all be used with small groups and most may be attempted with individual students. With the coming of mini-schools, open classrooms, and the growing participation of parents, paraprofessionals and teaching aides in the classroom, there will thankfully be less need for pre-planned group assignment-making and more work given over to individual bents.

This catalogue represents a major aspect of our work in schools—Assignments. They comprise one broad way of attempting to stimulate and encourage student writing. Some of our writers and teachers never use any of these ideas; each, however, has an "approach" (not a method or curriculum design) based on his sensitivity and interests in the teaching of writing. One writer says, "Locate the obsession, in the children directly, or in their poems. And watch carefully, because the obsession changes day to day."

Another says, "Sense the mood of the class." Another, "Don't come in with any preconceived plan." And still another, "I start with a specific assignment, but I abandon it as soon as we (the class and I) discover a more interesting direction."

We are ever still learning about the process of teaching. We will never develop a Method. We will still be asking the questions: How do you decide what to do in class? What do you do when an exercise isn't working? If the clues are always in the students, how do you look for and identify them?

In this catalogue, we have categorized ideas, we have labeled exercises for the convenience of this presentation, we have tried to include the many predilections of our writers and some of the endless interests of children. We encourage all teachers to break open the headings, find exceptions to the generalizations, trust their intuitions rather than these prescriptions, and constantly have their own accidental discoveries.

These are some of our discoveries, some ways into writing for enjoyment, writing what students care about, writing with their own voices and not merely mimicking the voice of their textbook poet or the voice they think the teacher wants to hear.

Some friends call this catalogue a bunch of recipes. It is. If so, we say, before you start cooking, find out what your class is hungry for. Store away the information of this book in your mind and use whatever you can whenever you think the time is right; use it to set off other associations leading to new ideas.

Just this past week, our twenty writers and countless teachers began with a hundred new approaches and ideas. No precepts here; except perhaps a liking for young people's writing and the classic needs of teaching (though it's been said many times, many ways)—a love of self and of those you teach.

Martin Kushner

Notes

This catalogue is a gathering of the work of many people; when we do not quote directly from the diaries of writers, the voice that speaks is the consensus of the Teachers & Writers staff.

We refer in this book to "children," "young people," "kids" and "students." There's no good word in our language that takes in all young people from the ages of 4 to 18. "Children" has the mildest sound, so we use it the most. But we set no ages upon these exercises and leave their uses to you—the teachers and writers.

Assignments

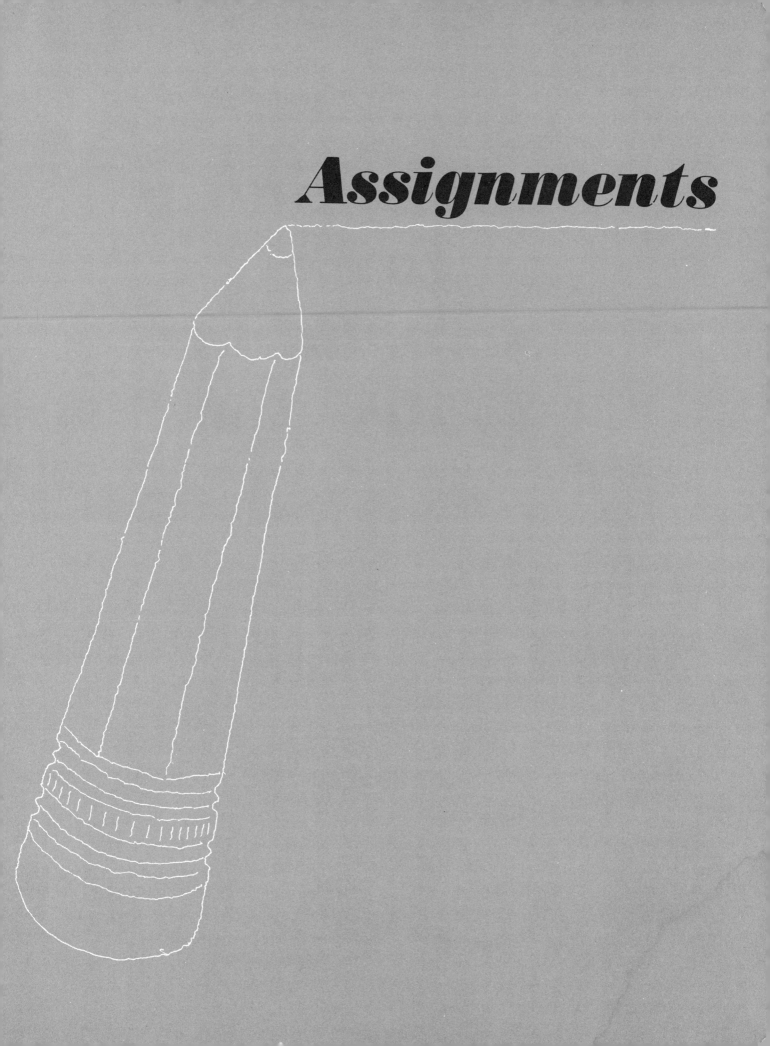

On Imagining To Be Something You're Not

Getting into another person's skin, taking an opposite point of view, going on holiday from the blinkered everyday self, becoming an apple on the tree, being in another man's shoes—these are leaps of the imagination common to all children and a wellspring for writers of all ages.

Children love to impersonate, mimic, act out, dress up. Children and adolescents daydream; they imagine themselves to be their heroes, to become the characters of their wishes. How does one allow a new character, a whole other human being, to possess them—to feel what that character feels, to see what he sees, to sense the life of another person without judging him—an act of generosity that can be so satisfying. How can one encourage and help young writers go beyond mimicry or stereotyping, in order to write in another persona—a character they would like to be or someone they hate or someone they fear. Without this movement toward compassion, many of the following ideas easily stop at joking or degenerate into facile "Hello, I'm a sunbeam" exercises.

At the younger age level, children have a strong sense of privacy and don't always like to touch on unhappy personal subject matter in their writing. It is often easier for them to express themselves through a mask, whether it be play acting, with a costume and an actual mask, or through an assumed narrative voice.

When someone is writing in another persona, it is important to stress that he search for the speech, the unique voice of that person. Novelist John Hawkes planned a whole year's work in Freshman Composition at Stanford (see Books Section for Baumbach's *Writer As Teacher*) around the attempt to make his students sensitive to the verbal style in which people speak—their idiosyncratic vocabulary, inflections, habitual subject matter—with the ultimate purpose of having them begin to define and develop and enrich their own writing voices.

MET...PHOSES

Bob Clawson explains an assignment he and poet Anne Sexton gave to their high school class:

"The assignment was this: You wake up and you're something in the refrigerator... Then we decided to write on this challenge: 'I woke up as a giant insect.' We followed that with Kafka's 'Metamorphosis,' and ... a reading of Jeff Brown's *Flat Stanley*. After that, we had them write about waking up in a ...dicine cabinet, then waking up as an old man or an ...oman, then waking up as a member of the ...osite sex, their age."

B... AN ANIMAL OR A THING

"Children feel close to animals and objects, close enough to talk to them, close enough to identify with them. Without much difficulty they can imagine what it feels like to be a dog, a fish, a teddy bear, a cloud, or a piano. This is one of the great fundamental poetic talents, and children have more of it than adults. ... In asking for poems about animals and things, I suggested they imagine they were the animal or thing and write from that point of view. A few examples in class are a good way to get them in a happy and identifying state of mind: How would it feel to be a TV set? I would have a big, blank face. Then there would be music and lights inside me. I didn't insist that the poems show complete identification with the object or animal, and in fact some are dialogues, some are written from the outside, some are half inside half outside. What I wanted, so the children would get the most from these poems, was that they feel for the subjects rather than merely observe them."

(from Kenneth Koch's *Wishes, Lies and Dreams*)

TALKING JISMOES

This is a play idea used with a fourth grade by poet Dick Gallup.

"I had the class dictate things to me, and these things were to be the 'characters' of our play. I explained that the things would be able to talk and behave like people. The list gave me just about what I had in mind: a can of green beans, a can of blue beans, a spoon, a fork, a banana, a mouth, and a narrator, which they added at the end of the play. The play itself worked out very well."

BIOGRAPHY OF SOMEONE IN CLASS

Phillip Lopate tried this idea on a class the first day of school, but it can be used with any group:

"I had been mulling over a delightful assignment: to write the biography (or autobiography) of the person sitting next to you. What better opportunity, before they knew more than a few details about each other. They were all strangers, meeting for the first time, and I explained that they would have to go on non-verbal clues: dress, posture, face. It was like staring at someone in the subway and imagining his life. They could invent any damn thing they wanted, even carry the biography to the very end (I told them I liked death scenes in biographies). They set to work. I noticed several cackling to themselves. It was an opportunity for outrageous mischief. ...

"I was a little alarmed at the degree of malice and condescension that strangers greet each other with, but for me the best written pieces were those which genuinely allowed the malice to flow."

THE PERSON YOU HATE

You become the person you hate most, not necessarily a specific individual but a physical or personality type that most offends you (the bully, the sniveler, the fop). You become that character, not in order to pass judgment, but to discover the forces which motivate him/her. Combine movement or dramatic improvisations with your attempt: try walking like this person, dancing like this person on a happy day in his life, on a sad day; try to discover what experiences make him joyful or despairing; get a dialogue going between several of these hateful types.

MY FRIEND AMERICA

Personify some large abstraction or institution (Infinity, Beauty, Chicago, God, Mississippi) and write about it as if it were a person you know very well.

Poet Doughtry Long writes: "I asked the students to describe America, only I told them to use the characteristics and personality of a fellow classmate. Again they were told to use lies, exaggerate, etc. The results were fascinating, particularly when the personal idiosyncrasies began to take on the aspects of a national character."

WEIRD VOICES

One way of sharpening the concept of voice is to go to extremes. Write in the voice of an insane person (as in Gogol's famous story, "Diary of a Madman") or someone with a stutter or without any front teeth, or someone who doesn't know the language very well. Again, the purpose is not to make fun of, but to take on the experience of another.

EAVESDROP

The old favorite assignment for creative writing students who commit atrocities in the name of written dialogue is to send them out with a pad and pencil to eavesdrop. It can't take more than ten minutes to discover how people *don't* talk (smoothly, in full sentences, with complex syntax, answering questions directly). Discovering how they *do* talk is a good bit harder and varies with about the same frequency as fingerprints. There is also the practical problem that kids can't write all that fast if they're trying to get down everything they hear. But it's worth trying and there's certainly nothing more fun than sanctioned spying.

—Rosellen Brown

FAMILIAR STORIES FROM ANOTHER ANGLE

Little Red Riding Hood told from the wolf's point of view. (It is helpful to begin this exercise by telling stories aloud.) Around Christmas time, writer Cristy Noyes asked her class to tell the Nativity from the point of view of anyone or anything in the vicinity—the shepherd, the star, the cow, Joseph. . . . This is an excellent way of introducing students to the dynamics of story-telling. (See also Merle Chianese's account of working from a newspaper clipping in OUTSIDE CATALYSTS, p. 14.)

THE DREAMS OF OTHERS

A direct way of getting into another person's brain is to imagine what his sleeping or waking fantasies might be like. Write about the dreams of others:

The blind man dreams of a sparkler

The egg dreams of an omelette

The nose dreams of its glasses

The inspector dreams of inspection day

The soda dreams of its pop

CATHY MAITLAND: CHARACTERS

1. Sun
2. Stamp Machine
3. Apple
4. Zaz Zaz Gabor
5. Myself

ACT I

This story begins at 4:30 AM. The scene, a large bowl in which the Sun sleeps. "Boy, am I tired," says the Sun at 5:00 AM. He gets out of bed and puts on his yellow coat and begins to get up. At about 7:30 he's half up, looking at the early risers watching him. At 12:00 noon he's as high as he can go. He burns off all the energy he has and about 3:00 begins to go down the other way. At about 6:00 PM he gets back into bed and stores up energy for tomorrow.

ACT II

I am a stamp machine. I can stamp up to $25.00 if I want to. But mostly I stamp 6¢ which isn't much. I feel that cold envelope come into my body and then hit it as hard as I can. When my stamp starts to get low, they fill me up again, and I'm ready to go.

ACT III

I love being an apple on an apple tree. Sometimes when it's hot I just hang on to my house and get bigger and redder, but sometimes someone comes along and takes one of my loved ones away. Then they take me too and eat me all up and then I'm gone. But all my friends are there to carry on.

ACT IV

I am the pretty Zaz Zaz. I am pretty, but I lead a lonely life. I am getting old and my many husbands are all gone, and really, I guess I'm not that pretty anymore. I guess it's time for Ava to take my place.

ACT V

I am myself. I live in a world of reality and dreams. My dreams are both happy and sad, and I also know I must face reality. I love life and most of the things in it. I hope some day to be a good wife and mother. But, before, I hope to model.

Cathy Maitland
Julia Richman High School
New York City

I woke up one morning very cold. I could not understand why. I assumed that the sun had not come up yet because everything was pitch black. I strained to see my watch but I could not find it, I could not even feel my hand or arm. They were gone. I wondered if I had any legs for I could not feel them, lacking hands. Here I noticed that hands were more important than legs because you need hands to feel legs. Trying to sit up the feeling of a cold plastic bag came across my face. Just then I heard a loud noise and a flash of light appeared. Frantically looking around I saw that I was a piece of celery and was being kept in a refrigerator. A hand approached me and clasped me among four other delicacies. We were then placed on a plate where I observed what was going on. The kitchen was familiar, it was our kitchen. I could see my mother scurrying along preparing the meal. Just then my father came in and sat down in front of me. Looking down I could see the reflection of me in his eyes. I was rather tall and the top of me looked like Paul Bruce's haircut. That's all there was, hair and trunk. My father picked me up and I tried to yell, but there was no sound. I tried to move but there was no movement. His mouth opened and half my trunk was engulfed. The pain was unbearable. Another bite and my head was the only thing left with Bruce's lousy hair on it. I thought to myself, I have been decapitated from the bottom up.

Brad
Wayland High School, Mass.

ONASSIS' YACHT

I'm Onassis' yacht. Last month Mr. Onassis and his family had a trip. They took me so far away. When they got there, they left me so far from them. They took other people with them. It was too overloaded for me. When they came back I was suffering because I was freezing. The water was so cold! Also the sharks were bothering me and biting me. When they got back, Mr. Onassis didn't repair me. I felt very tired. I didn't know how I could stay all night in the water. Oh my god, how much I suffered! It was terrible! Next day, Mr. Onassis came to me. He swept me and cleaned me very well. After he did all of these things I felt happy, thought I was going to rest, but it wasn't like I was thinking. The same day they planned another trip. This time they were going to have a party on the water. They were going to keep me two days resisting this stuff. So I had to be in the habit of traveling every time they wanted to.

Since Mr. Onassis bought me, I haven't had any repose. The worst thing in the world is to be a yacht.

Elsie Pagan
ROC High School
New York City

THE GERBIL

You are a gerbil. In a pet store. Running around in dirty wood shavings, longing for freedom. People come. They stare. They look. They poke. They say no. A man comes in. He looks. He pokes. He says yes. He takes you to a place. In a cardboard box. It is opened. Other people come and look. They poke. You are taken out and put in a maze of blocks. You hurry in, out. People look in. They stare. They stare for a long time. They take notes. This goes on. You are moved to another place. There, more people stare. Some laugh. They stare. They stare. You are in the maze. The blocks change. You hurry in and out of them, trying to get free. The blocks change. You hurry in, out. You are near insanity. The blocks change. You scurry in, out. The blocks change. You scurry in, out. The blocks change. You scurry in, out. The blocks change. You hurry in, out. The blocks change. You scurry in, out. The blocks change. You DIE. YOU DIE. YOU DIE. YOU DIE.

Jennifer Wada
8th Grade
Clinton Program, New York City

ROBERTO CLEMENTE'S BAT

I am Roberto Clemente's bat. He takes me every day and hurts me badly when he uses me to hit the ball. When I can't hit the ball, he furiously throws me on the ground and kicks me. When his time comes to go to home plate, I start to cry, but the only thing that I love is when he waves me because I feel like a bird—free.

David Ayala
ROC High School
New York City

Like most professional writers, children sometimes clutch when confronted with the blank page, and need something from outside to get their imaginations going. Many of the following ideas have long been standard creative writing procedures—others are fairly new—but all are addressed to the need, at times, for catalysts and surprises in the classroom.

Outside Catalysts

WRITING TO MUSIC

Anything goes, depending on the teacher's individual tastes. It helps to choose a piece because you love it, rather than because it would seem to make good "program music," since kids pick up quickly on excitement or contempt. The writing might be anything—a dream, a memory, stream-of-consciousness, monster stories evoked by contemporary electronic music.

TOUCHING, SMELLING, TASTING

Set out on the desk a battery of things with interesting surfaces to be touched by a blindfolded child.

Make it clear that the point is not to try to identify the object, but to say what it feels like, what it makes him think of or remember.

Encourage him to search for many associations, unusual "synaesthetic" descriptions—crossings-over from one sense to another, such as "this grater feels like my dog barking."

The same can be done with tasting, by pushing words like sweet and sour into greater concreteness, or with a series of smells.

With all these the blindfold (or eyes shut) makes a difference: it prevents distraction and enforces concentration on the essences of the things at hand.

This can be viewed as an exercise in metaphor, complete in itself, or used as a jumping-off place for writing about memory.

—Rosellen Brown

WRITING TO PICTURES

Using magazines such as *Life, Ebony, National Geographic*, etc., pick out interesting photos, minus captions, give them to the kids, and ask them to write a poem or story to accompany the picture (i.e., what's going on?).

Reproductions of modern art, and especially personal photographs—families, vacations, portraits—might be useful too.

FOUND POEMS

You find the poems. It's that simple. Take any printed page in a book: what does the eye fall on? The first phrase the eye hits, use. Then skip, link it with anything else that makes sense. Keep going, like that, until, by accident, a series of accidents, you've created—rather you've served as tour guide in creating—a "found" poem. It was there already; you simply brought the elements together.

—Clarence Major

Another way of going about it is to have the children select a text from a non-poetic source, such as the newspaper, and arrange the prose in short lines to form a poem.

CUTOUTS

Cut out words from magazines, make a pile of them, and glue them down in any order on a clean sheet of paper. Even where the pieces are not "meaningful" to adult readers, there is always interest in the individual words and phrases.

PROPS

Various writers and teachers have brought in:

feathers	a bar of soap
African masks	medieval tapestries
mice	old shoes

and used them successfully as spurs to the imagination.

Children can describe the thing, its feelings, where it came from, or make up a story about it.

Bring in a whole collection of ordinary and unusual objects, set them out on a table; let the kids choose one or more objects to write about.

INVISIBLE WRITING

Lemon juice is best and easiest; or you can use iron sulphate to write with and washing soda dissolved in water to bring out the writing.

Use a Q-tip or toothpick or an old-fashioned straight pen to write with (not any point that will make an impression).

When the writing is dry, hold it over a source of heat—a very warm radiator, a steaming toaster, or, most convenient, a bulb of at least 150 watts left on long enough to heat up. The juice will turn brown almost instantly.

After they've finished simply sending sinister messages, kids can concoct a story in which an invisible message is a crucial part.

—Rosellen Brown

CAPTIONS

Either kids can find their own pictures to caption, or the teacher can supply them. It's endlessly suggestive to find pictures of people talking to each other (or in similar unspecific relation) and caption the picture with what they might be saying.

You can also use comic books and comic strips: paint out the words in the balloons (with white poster paint) and have the kids fill in the dialogue.

MAKING COMIC BOOKS

I carried a shopping bag full of the contraband that I had to sneak out of my house and into the school. Fanning out a handful of the books was enough to snap them to lively attention.

From the talk triggered, I learned that the world of comics was built on a complex structure of characterization, plot, locale and legend. These kids were all aficionados of this literature, and partisan to particular publishers, lines and heroes.

After talking up this whirlwind, we brought the talk around to action. I proposed that we create new characters and scenes. We talked of some types we could create, that could accomplish any of our hopes.

Some characters that were imagined were: MARKO PORKO—the boy who could eat his way out of any situation; HIP MAN—the man with powers to freak anybody out; SUPERSPADE—a black man whose special powers were used to set things right for his people.

—Art Berger

Lennox Raphael also found that kids took to making comics:

"Kids do relate in a very alive way to visual involvement and I saw the making of comic books as one very effective method of loosening them up and breaking down the great fear (out of respect and confusion) of the printed word. Print. They were being harnassed to print and judged by it too—at a time like this when mixed media remain unexploited in the classroom."

POETRY CHARADES

The teacher or a student performs four or five charades—simple physical gestures—all of which should be very mysterious and unidentifiable; the class writes down what it makes them think of, using complete sentences.

While the charades are not necessarily related, the sentences written by the class should be; otherwise it gets too fragmentary.

Here is an account of one such assignment:

"I gave a few examples, such as extending my arms to my right and left respectively, with finger pointing . . . then gradually moved them toward each other, until they met in front of me . . . the extended fingers approaching each other until they touched and then 'exploded'—I made my hands fly up explosively. What is that? 'Two airplanes crashing in mid-air,' 'Two electric plugs touching,' etc. Then I told them they had to make it a whole 'thing,' like a sentence, to tell me everything: what kind of airplanes, what color, why did they crash, what was in the planes, etc. . . .

"This was one level of the assignment: a sort of dance. I tried to tune them in to another scene, whereby they would watch what I was doing, and write about how it made them feel, not just what they thought it was. I'm afraid this is somewhat harder, if more desirable, because the kids love charades. . . .

"I'm not sure I was terribly successful in getting them to write great poems, but there was a lot of nice feeling in the class, 100 per cent interest in the assignment, and some imagination unleashed. As for their writing complete sentences, I'm afraid it was all too interesting to remember that dictum; still, some beautiful pieces. . . ."

—Ron Padgett

TAKING OFF FROM NEWS STORIES

Merle Chianese approached a class of fourth graders this way:

"I read them a newspaper story, which was a factual, non-human-interest account of a student riot in Manila in which the students, demonstrating in support of transportation workers on strike, threw rocks at buses and taxis, burned a professor's car, and threw home-made bombs. The police wounded forty-one and killed three students, the professor shot at and wounded a student, and the riot eventually was contained when student leaders were arrested."

After discussing with the class the possible reasons for the conflict, ". . . I then said that newspaper writing demanded a clear, logical, unfeeling approach, so that people could learn the facts, but only the facts—the who, what, where, how. . ., but that the WHY belonged to the province of the creative writer—the reasons, the feelings that people have.

"I asked them to imagine that they were really there—not in the class reading about it on page 15, safe and comfortable, not at home reading the paper after dinner, not listening to a teacher describing something far away—but really and truly there—they might be a student demonstrating, a student throwing a bomb, a student sympathetic to the cause but not quite ready for violence, a cop, a cop with kids at college, a fireman, a nurse, a teacher, the teacher who shot the student, a bus driver on strike or scabbing, a passenger on a bus being stoned . . . or even a little puppy dog lost in the melée. Think about it. What does it look like, sound like, feel like? What do bombs do?"

LITERARY MODELS

Sometimes the work of young people can deepen immeasurably after the exposure to serious, quality poetry and prose.

Very important is that we all teach what we enjoy, what interests us, and not because we need to cover the classics, or expose children to masterpieces that we never much cared for ourselves.

"The best way to teach black kids to write is to bring in large doses of

Gwendolyn Brooks   Langston Hughes

Don L. Lee   Nicholas Guillen
Sonia Sanchez   Mari Evans

These are contemporary poets, from them we can get to the great heritage of black literature. From the particular and familiar of contemporary black poets and writers we can capture the enthusiasm of the young student and really begin to teach."

—David Henderson

"I introduce the idea of writing about an imaginary world. I say that today we just want to talk and write about ways to get there. . . .

"I point out that a lot of people have written about imaginary worlds, and that until about a hundred years ago the way they usually got there was by boat. There would be a storm, they would get lost, and suddenly find themselves in a place no one had ever discovered before. I say that today we have many different ways of traveling to such a place, and ask the kids for ideas.

"They respond immediately with enthusiasm: submarine, space-ship, airplane, you could get hijacked. Then I asked if there are ways of traveling in your own head—'dreams, imagination.' You could also travel into the future, one kid says. Great! Does he know a book called *The Time Machine*? He does. I say that I had planned to read a few pages from it today. We turn out the lights and turn on the record player—Eliot Carter's *Double Concerto* which I describe as imaginary world music—too bad for Carter. I read from the opening pages of Wells' book. . . .

"Then I ask the kids to return to their desks to write about their own ways of traveling to an imaginary place."

from *Imaginary Worlds*,
—by Richard Murphy, published
by Teachers & Writers.

Children especially like their own literature. They like to read the work of their classmates; they like to hear and read stories and poems by other children. They enjoy discussing their own literature and writing for an appreciative audience of their peers.

Make lots of other literature available. Have it around. Read from works you like. Share your enthusiasm for what you like and enjoy the kids enjoying the writing that excites or interests them. Help them to it. Heaping tables-full of it.

THE GRANDADDY OUTSIDE CATALYST OF THEM ALL

Bring a live writer into your room!

(Written to Greek Bazouki Music)

This reminds me of a dancing centipede. The rhythm you hear is made by his feet elbows and friends. He has at least 8,000,678,876 feet. He is a very good dancer. His friend the bird makes the music sometimes with his wings, he flies with rhythm. Sometimes his other friend the Lippizan horse dances ballet and keeps in rhythm with the music. Sometimes his friend the cow puts in a mooooooooow or two. Sometimes it's made from the raindrop in the back of a whale's throat, also sometimes it is made from his spout too.

Amy Gelber
5th Grade
P. S. 75, New York City

(Found Poem)

In San Francisco
Westinghouse propulsion and control systems
will be the heart of BART
75 miles of subway, surface
and elevated rail lines.
Automatic
hands off operation.

Six and a half million people are moved
in and around New York
daily
More than half
of the subway cars
have Westinghouse propulsion equipment

Similar Westinghouse systems
will power the advanced transit network designed for
San Paulo, Brazil, the hemisphere's
second largest city.

We also think smaller.

Westinghouse Ad

My heart beats like a bat in a
baseball game
And like the thumping of the rain
And like a tornado whirling a rock
at a house.

The End

Michael Ormiston
3rd Grade
Horace Mann School
Bayonne, New Jersey

SOUNDS

The door sounds like a mouse
getting his tooth filled.
Your heart beating sounds like
someone knocking at the door.
A plant said to Miss McHugh,
"You don't water me enough."

Joan Korba
5th Grade

THE TYPEWRITER

A typewriter sounds like tap dancing
sounds like Walter Cronkite eating corn on the cob.
sounds like a mother giving a lecture
or a teacher hitting you with a ruler
it sounds like turkish fleas
it sounds like the boys' bellybuttons going in and out
it sounds like the slaves blowing their noses
it sounds like two eggs cracking.

Group Poem
5th Grade

WHEN I CLOSE MY EYES

When I close my eyes I always see
fat, little men with stripes
And they always march to the
toothpick battle.
But when they try to run,
They always fall down and roll
like a berry
on their stomachs.

Lew Schultz
P. S. 75, New York City

15

Magic: Black and Otherwise

by Marvin Hoffman

Every time I see a batch of children's work I am struck by the unbalanced, biased picture it paints of what goes on in children's heads. And every attempt to compensate for the omissions creates a new kind of imbalance. Thus when books like *Wishes, Lies and Dreams* and *Miracles* were published they were (explicitly or implicitly) attempts to demonstrate that children could write beautifully and with humor about their inner selves and about what they observed in the world around them. None of these qualities was evident in the work coming out of most classrooms.

But now it looked as if children were funny, silly, wistful and innocent creatures. There was nothing intentional about the concept of childhood which emerged; it was a necessary side effect of righting some other wrongs.

All of which is a roundabout way of saying that I have another weight to throw on the balance. I think that children's fantasies and imaginations are filled with magic, sometimes "funny, cute" magic, but as often as not, magic of a very sinister variety. Children are very interested in power, which is not surprising when you consider that they are probably the most defenseless, powerless group in human society. People bigger and stronger than they are persist in doing things to them from which there is no recourse. So a lot of thought goes into revenge, secret sources of power, and supernatural ways of getting the edge on other people. This past year I began experimenting with some forms and subjects that might provide an outlet for these more "sinister" imaginings, as well as for lighter kinds of magic. Several other writers with the Collaborative, among them Phillip Lopate, have been working in a similar vein.

HYPNOTISM

A very heady bit of magic, since it places someone under your control, subject to your commands. Initially I turned the idea into a formula poem where each line began "I command you to. . ." or "You must. . ." Actually the idea is powerful enough to carry itself after a preliminary discussion of hypnosis and hypnotism.

As with most writing ideas, the examples you begin with are all-important. My initial examples were too cute, smacked too much of the adult pretending to be a child: "You must bring me an ice-cream soda every day at 3 o'clock"—that sort of thing. It didn't encourage the darker impulses but a lot of "illicit" commands emerged nonetheless: orders to rob, to kill, to do harm to oneself. (The thing that fascinated me most about hypnotism when I was a kid was those people who obeyed orders to burn themselves and stick pins in their hands.)

By the way, this idea worked equally well as an individual or as a collaborative effort. It's also been suggested that very young children who don't know about hypnotism can have a good time—minus the darker overtones—playing "Simon Says" with the wildest orders they can muster.

INVISIBILITY

An equally powerful idea which forms the basis for countless fairy tales and myths is the idea of invisibility. If you could conceal yourself you could go anywhere, be part of the situations you have previously been locked out of, wreak all sorts of havoc without having to pay the consequences, even be a secret benefactor.

I never got beyond encouraging simple poems which consisted of one line listings of what you would do if you were invisible. Again there were lots of bank robberies, food thefts, undetected wallops, plus a good deal of sneaking around in people's bedrooms. The idea is more expandable than this; it should be no problem moving into larger and more varied forms around this theme: stories, fairy tales, narrative poems, etc.

A kindred idea which I got from Betty Kline, a teacher in Springfield, Ohio, is X-RAYS. Again, the name conjures up such possibilities that there was no need to discuss forms or anything else. Here is a sample of what emerged:

X-RAYS

Your heart isn't big enough
To see.
It's as big as a fist.
Why is it as big as a fist?

Our teacher
We called her Miss Freckleface
Because she had freckles on
Her face
And she brought a pig's heart
For science.

We went to a museum
And saw a transparent woman.
The things they talked about
Lit up.

When we went to the fair
We saw a little man.
He said, "Can I help you?"
But I was scared.
I turned my head.

> *Dean, Robin, Gary*
> *Gloria and Joseph*
> *Hayward Junior High School*
> *Springfield, Ohio*

SUPERSTITIONS

Young people of all ages have a fascination for things which bring good luck or bad luck. (For that matter I know few adults who don't harbor some very primitive superstitions in the form of rituals, omens, talismans, which bring good fortune and ward off the bad.) I have tried making the double-columned lists of things that bring good luck and things that bring bad luck. Once you work your way past the cultural cliches—black cats, ladders, broken mirrors—which are so universally believed that they have lost their mythic force, you enter a fascinating realm of cultural traditions, family inheritances and private fantasies. What emerges here are fundamental beliefs about birth and death, sickness and health, wholeness and deformity, madness, the interpretation of dreams. There's no place you can't go from here—poems, stories, plays, anthropology. One inspired fifth-grader even took her good-luck/bad-luck list and turned it into a board game.

CHARMS AND WITCHCRAFT

A special subspecies of superstitions which, once again, abounds in fairy tales, folklore and mythology—rabbit's feet, lucky pennies, amulets, love potions, voodoo dolls, hexes. I once showed some students a book called *Folk Beliefs of the Southern Negro* (Newbell Niles Puckett, Dover Paperback), an incredibly encyclopedic collection of charms, curses and cures which was compiled in the 1920's. We came to a particularly graphic description of charms capable of driving your adversary insane ("Get a hair from your enemy's head. Place it in a cloth along with some paper with his name on it. Nail it to a tree which he passes every day and he will go mad by sunrise.") One boy in the class scurried off for a pencil and paper and carefully copied down the instructions, partly in jest but partly out of a very serious intent to try it out. It was one of the incidents which convinced me that children were deeply concerned with finding ways to undo their tormentors, of which this particular student had many.

This whole area is one that can be treated objectively, by focusing on recording the charms which the students believe in or which they have found to be part of the beliefs of children and adults they know. Or it can be treated "fantastically" through the creation of stories and poems involving curses, charms, hexes. Stories about witches and other super-human or sub-human creatures revolve around the exercise of these magical powers to harm or to help ordinary mortals.

GHOSTS AND MONSTERS

Elementary school children rarely need encouragement to write stories of this genre. In fact the problem is often the opposite: how to turn off the flow or channel it in some new direction. I find that my tolerance for stories about Dracula, vampires, werewolves, Godzilla, and assorted monsters from outer space is low. There's nothing wrong with the subject—in fact they're good early subjects for kids who are uncomfortable with writing—but invariably the stories are stereotyped, formula pieces which are so predictable to both reader and writer that they require even less thought than the "How I Spent My Weekend" compositions. Kids are fully capable of creating their own fantastic monsters if they are encouraged to go beyond their banal TV characters, perhaps even to caricature those well-known monsters.

Worth noting: the Spring-Summer 1971 issue of *Foxfire* (see section on magazines) contains a wonderful thirty-six-page collection of "real" ghost stories which children should enjoy.

CURES, HOME REMEDIES

Another subject with mythic or humorous possibilities, depending on how you choose to treat it. I enjoyed collecting with students descriptions of cures and home remedies in use in their families: teas, powders, herbs, external applications. But some more light-hearted students spoofed the whole subject by inventing their own home cures, with results that approach Disgusting Menus.

WEATHER

I've never been able to do anything with this, since city kids are notoriously oblivious to natural phenomena, but if you're someplace where people are in closer touch with the elements, try recording beliefs about predicting the weather. ("If the bees store more honey than usual, it will be a long winter.") Obviously, the kids can create their own fantastic predictions to befuddle the local farmers. Eric Sloane has compiled an excellent collection of this weather lore, and *Foxfire* has a compendium in a recent issue.

TAROT CARDS

Fortune-telling is another realm of the supernatural to which children are naturally attracted—reading palm lines, deciphering kabbalistic number combinations, etc. For this reason tarot cards are fascinating material for a variety of writing activities. Most decks consist of beautifully colored, illustrated cards which come with detailed instructions for use as a fortune-telling device. It is possible to teach students to lay out the cards so that they are able to write their own or their classmates' fortunes. The cards can be used individually, rather than in patterns, as stimuli for fantastic story-writing. Here is an example of the latter use of tarot cards from the diaries of Merle Chianese:

I showed the class a deck of tarot cards and gave them a brief account of its history, explained that good fortune tellers did not use a set of standard meanings but bounced the pictures around in their head, unleashed the subconscious and made up a story about the person. I told them good storytellers did the same thing. Gave each child two cards, told them to study the pictures, look for meanings, ideas, feelings, stories. (It's a French deck so they couldn't get clues from the captions.) They started working immediately. They were a little uptight about whether their ideas were valid, but they were reassured that spelling, neatness, etc. didn't count, that I didn't give marks, and that what I cared about was that they have FUN. They wrote with abandon.

THE SKELETON

This skeleton is about to kill a guy. You can tell by what he's holding in his hand. He is going to chop a life, not wheat. A skeleton symbolizes death. He is going to chop through many lives. Kill! Grind! Rip! Tear! Snarl! (Gasp!) Ugh! Urk! Now the wheat (I mean lives) is cut.

Edward Rosen
5th Grade, P. S. 75
New York City

IN WALDBAUM'S

The last time I saw Dracula he was in Waldbaum's. He eats human's food—hamburgers, french fries, steak and milk. He was stealing them in Waldbaum's. People were afraid to say anything.

4th-Grade Student
P. S. 75, New York City

Mitchell, you are in my power.
Go jump in the river.
Sing like a bird.
You are a pig, go in the mud.
You are getting beautiful.

You are hypnotized.
You are getting sleepy.
Now you are dead.
You are a Peter Cottontail.

You are getting a punch in the nose.
You are awake, click, click, click.
Give me lots of colored diamonds.
You are Bozo the clown,
Fun, fun, fun.

Philip Micele

I would send you up Mt. Everest. You would climb and climb. You would be so tired. Up, up, up. But you just can't make it. But still the people start screaming at you "Go on, you make us work, now we are making you work!" But you can't make it. When you just fall down into the ice and rock. When suddenly you are being dragged. You suddenly feel very cold. We made it to the top they scream. But just when you are going to rest, they say "Time to go down." Ohhhh! you sigh and down down down you go. When you suddenly wake up in a bed. Many people are looking at you, many who work for you. You mutter some words. Everybody starts covering their mouths. They run out of the hospital and start screaming. And that's why people have vacations.

Ellen Feldman
P. S. 75, New York City

I am going to torture my brother. I will put him in a room with knives sticking out. Right behind him is a big cake. If he moves, he gets scratched.

Jonathan Friedman
P. S. 75, New York City

GOING HOME FROM SCHOOL

The trees sway like someone
Following you in a black coat
With a switchblade and a derby
With one hand in his pocket
Like a hook
And his name is Hookerman
He opens cans with his ears
He eats toenails and onions
And he sings out Hallelujah
There is a slit in his neck
And his bone goes through his nose
When he talks electricity wires spark
And his bark is worse than his bite.

Class Collaboration
4th Grade
Wharton, New Jersey

The purpose of this section is to encourage children as writers to connect with the concrete and unique in their own lives. All expressive writing, whether based on imagination or fact, is in a sense autobiographical. But here we're literally emphasizing feelings, memories, and direct perceptions about the present. Placing importance on expressing personal feelings helps a child place importance on himself.

Personal Writing

I REMEMBER

I asked the kids, what's the first thing you remember, when you were very little—not what your parents told you but what you yourself recall. Some mentioned animals, accidents, sickness, learning to swim and being afraid of drowning. The natural drift was toward stranger and scarier memories. In the end kids were reporting having seen the devil and having been kissed by angels.

There was a surprising (for this class) amount of attentiveness to each other's stories. After 45 minutes when everyone's memories were churning, I distributed paper, suggesting either a poem with each line beginning I Remember, or a story, leaving it very open-ended.

Another time I brought in scents (lemon, sandalwood soap) and asked the kids to associate memories from different smells. A useful starter.

David Shapiro has an interesting variant of I Remember: Have the kids lie down, turn off the lights, and pretend they are remembering for a psychiatrist!

Phillip Lopate

I began by asking the class to write down their memories . . . because I think that memories are very close to what one is, and somehow very close to the creative source of things.

"In my country . . ." wrote Deyanira Dela Cruz. She began story after story. She asked me words, how to spell them. She knew the words. She seemed to shine with these memories and with the joy of writing, learning.

Her teacher was amazed. She said Deyanira had not been able to concentrate on anything else since she'd been in the class. She wrote all afternoon, and through the free period too.

Hannah Green

Traumas: The most scary or silly or embarrassing experience in my life. . . .

NOTHING

I'm sitting here doing nothing just rotting away trying to write something. But now and then I get an idea but I just scrap it again and again. "I just can't think of anything," I say to myself, and go on again—but I finally got a good idea and try to write a little and presto!!! here is where I am up to writing all of this B————T!!!

My mind is wiped clean by this idiot who comes here once a week and sucks my head clean of ideas by putting my ideas on paper and printing them and handing them to other students for their knowledge enlargement.

The End
Matthew Johnson
6th Grade
P. S. 75, New York City

I want to stay here
It's so cool
My mind wonders into the coats
I look and it gets darker and darker
And then my mind just wants to stay there
In the furry inside of the coat
I start to relax
The furriness makes me want to go to sleep

I'm asleep

Mike Bezney
5th grade
Wharton, New Jersey

SAD

It feels like your whole life means nothing to you.
Sadness fills your heart.
You don't care what happens.
Your eyes fill with tears and your nose runs.
You don't feel like moving from the spot that you
        heard about it.
That day you will always remember that feeling you
        had inside you.
Sometimes you have gone crazy.
Your whole life has been changed.
Everywhere you go you won't get away from the
        feeling.
It just seems that you can't get away from it.
Somehow you will always remember that day.
It seems like it is stuck in your mind.
The mind is like a tape recorder.
Don't forget you can't get away from that feeling.

Mark Mull
5th Grade
Wharton, New Jersey

FEELINGS

On Friday I feel like jumping up and down and throwing confetti
On Friday night I could feel like killing myself, or like
        distributing champagne, or like filling a reservoir with bad water, or just plain empty.
At times I feel like walking on a meadow with someone
        who would be very close to me, or like those TV
        commercials about a guy and a girl.
Sometimes I feel like popping every little child's balloon.
Or at times I feel like just not existing.
This morning I smiled at everyone, and laughed at practically
        everything, while my friends looked at me
        in disbelief

Maria Castillo
Julia Richman High School
New York City

A PEACE OF SOFT THOUGHT

November, what a month to relax in.
Sweater, coats, and soft pink jackets.
Here I am sitting in school when all of a sudden
I thought I saw a martian, I did, I did, on a picture.
Bored, that's what I am, bored.
But what, isn't vacation what I want?
The leaves are turning, snow is falling, winter
growing, yes that is what I have and what I
want.

Lee Maidoff
6th Grade
P. S. 75, New York City

21

RECORD KEEPING

Time Capsules

Someone selects a half-hour from the day before and everyone writes everything he or she remembers about that half hour: what you did, what you felt, what you said, what you saw, what you thought. If you really get into it, it should take at least a half hour to write about a half hour. Suppose you were sleeping? Write about your dream.

—Norm Fruchter

Traditional Family Stories

Kids write down the stories they've grown up hearing (either realistic events or old-country "tales"). What if they asked their parents and grandparents for such stories and wrote them down, or taped and transcribed them? Vast stores of real and fabulous tale-telling are there for the asking.

Diaries

Anything students would like to preserve. If they seem to need an assurance of privacy, at least from time to time, urge them to write but not show what they've done, even to you. And respect their secrecy. Any breach of privacy will ruin your word, and justly so.

Reportage

Get the class into the habit of writing about anything out of the ordinary that happens—a trip, a fire, an ambulance, animals, giving birth, etc.

Scientific note-taking, carrying around a writer's notebook, carrying a camera, constantly jotting notes about experiences and thoughts is good for developing accurate observation and can only strengthen creative writing.

Letters

Love letters, letters of apology, letters thanking someone, letters to a celebrity.

Letters never mailed: to God, Santa Claus.

Serious letters to real people with power (electric company, the mayor, etc.)

Send postcards to names picked at random from the phone book.

Try writing a whole story through letters, as in epistolary novels like *Pamela* or *Les Liaisons Dangereuses*.

PLACE

How do you get a child to evoke a precise sense of place?

Rosellen Brown writes: "Suggest that he write about some place he knows or remembers very well—his own house, somewhere he spent a summer, Christmas at his grandparents', the country he was born in if he's not native-born, whatever he can write about in clear and rich detail. One might want to list details in unbroken flow, another might start every sentence with 'In my native country . . .' or 'My secret place is . . .' or 'On my block . . .' Or he might set a story there or write a descriptive piece. Whatever he does, encourage a choice of forms and great detail—colors, shapes, surfaces, sensations—and remind him of the possibilities of metaphor and simile."

HERE AND NOW

Stream of Consciousness

Set the right mood of quiet and concentration. Pick up a pencil and for five minutes write down everything that passes through your head. If you get distracted by something, include the distraction.

If you insist on having no thoughts, don't give up; instead write down everything around you.

Fool with words, and their sounds, what they lead to, nonsense and all, when you just relax into them. (See example from *In The Early World*. Bibliogrpahy p. 66.)

—Rosellen Brown

What I'd Really Like To Be Doing Right Now

An invitation to go anywhere out of this classroom. For those who still won't write, you might try asking them to explain—"Why I Don't Feel Like Writing." (See example of Matthew for its rare honesty.)

Classroom Awareness

Like Stream of Consciousness, but more specifically tied to the senses, here and now.

"Do you ever remember that you are alive?" Ron Padgett asked a class. "That you are here, sitting, breathing. To clarify what I meant, I mentioned how you forget you exist, when watching an absorbing movie. But to have the movie end! and you remember that you're in a theater, that the world is different than the screen, that you are you. . . .

"The kids, much to my surprise, seemed to dig this, and I had paper passed out while I asked them to write down what they see, hear, feel, smell, think, dream, RIGHT NOW. Example: I am sitting in my desk. (Not what happened a few minutes ago, or what will happen later, but right now.) Example: I have two eyes. I am listening. I am writing."

Poem To A Reader

Allan Feldman asked his class to write poems directly addressed to the anonymous reader.

This is an excellent way of attracting and keeping

an audience; knowing someone is there at the other end helps the writer to focus and to speak in a more direct, personal voice.

DREAMS

You can write about a dream, draw a dream or take it a step further by dramatizing a dream.

To avoid the flippant "but it was only my mother waking me for school" approach, encourage writing about the dream as direct experience, as if it really happened, even bypassing the label "dream."

BIRTH AND DEATH

Have you ever imagined your birth? What did you think about in the womb, at the moment of delivery, when you saw the doctor, when you were slapped and started to cry? Where were you before you were born? Many children, of course, have wild conceptions about their birth, with no idea of how it really happens—a delicate but joyous subject for exploration.

How do children imagine death? They write works which may strike an adult reader as morbid; they are often obsessed by images of death—from the squishing of a bug to the planet's extinction—that are too familiar for comfort. It is from this instinct, however, that the more interesting writing will come, the personal visions that rise above the accepted abstractions and cliches about death.

Imagine yourself dying: what does it feel like, what does it look like, what does it feel like to be dead—these questions may take the writers into the mythology of heaven and hell, devils, angels, and God. They could do a large mural of heaven and hell (like Bosch or Michelangelo).

Death is a subject that will arrive naturally in class out of the personal experiences of all of us—funerals, grandparents, memories of the process.

Suicide Notes is another interesting, grisly assignment, which gives the student a chance to express and, hopefully, transcend his feelings of self-pity. Another idea is to ask the class to write accounts imagining they had only twenty-four hours to live. The last diary entry.

MY DREAM

This happened a long time ago when I was little. I lived in my country. I heard that my grandfather was dead and I cried a lot. When it was time to go to bed, I thought of him, and when thinking of him, I felt sleepy and went to sleep, and I had a dream of my grandfather.

And in the morning my mother called to tell me the good news and my mother told me that it wasn't real that my grandfather had died, and I was so happy that I kissed my mother so much, and then mother told me to stop kissing her so much, that she has another surprise for me; and I asked her what was the surprise, and she opened the door and I couldn't believe that it was my grandfather.

And I told him what I heard, and he said I should go out and teach them a good lesson, and I told him I was so surprised that I kissed her so much.

Deyanira Dela Cruz
4th Grade
P. S. 41, New York City

MY DREAM

I only have good dreams. Once I had a dream about a candy store—a man came in and robbed it. My mother owned it. She got killed in the robbery. So I ate all of the candy in the store and bubble gum. I ate the french fries and the hamburger and some of the frankfurter. She had heroes and stuff like that. I became so full I had to have my stomach pumped. I kept on spitting up. The doctor said I should've came earlier because I need my tonsils out. I said "NO" I ate enough candy and stuff like that. He said I can die if I didn't have it out. I said let me die, let me die. They said, "No" we try to succeed in every patient. I said don't try to succeed in me. They said if it was up to me I wouldn't but it's not up to me so goodbye. They came in later—I was laying there pretending I was die. They put me in a casket. I was buried alive.

The End

P.S. I'm glad it wasn't true—the only part I wish was true is the part about the candy store and about the hamburgers and stuff.

Jackie Deas
P. S. 75
New York City

WHAT IT FEELS LIKE TO BE DEAD

It's like you don't exist
If you don't think you go crazy
And it seems like you don't have a brain
And it seems like you don't have a body
You're floating around in your coffin
Your brain is floating around
Looking for somebody else to go into
You're restless because you can't do anything
Your teeth fall out
Your eyes fall out and they dig a hole in the country
And then your retina
You get skinny
You stop growing
Because you don't eat anything
You eat the soil
Part of you comes off and it grows under the ground
And it grows into another person
But he's dead too
They take your blood out

When I saw my grandmother in her coffin
She had a red dress on
But when she died she was wearing pajamas
My stepfather was throwing up
Then his blood came rushing out of his stomach
And mixed with the throw-up.
The worms come into you
And they crawl inside you
The fish eats the worms
They go through the dead guy's eyeballs
But first they have the termites
To eat your coffin away
The termites pry open your stomach
And they take the food out of it
And they give some of the food to people who are dead
They eat the coffin
And the dead people come undead
They gay green light brings them to life

It feels like you're gushing around in there
When you're brought back to life
You have the pure joy of consciousness

> by the class
> Bedford—Lincoln MUSE
> Brooklyn, New York

WHEN I HAD A DREAM
OF A LOVE STORY

One day I was downstairs eating breakfast. My boyfriend came in and he kissed me and said let me have some coffee. OK I said, I made it, I said, and he said I need $30. I said what for Johnny, oh for something Rhoda—that was my name. I gave him the coffee and did not give him the money and he left and I went down stairs and I started to cry and then I woke up and it was a dream.

AND that goes to show you never trust nobody not even your own boyfriend.

The End

> By you know who
> Dolores Velez
> P. S. 75, New York City

The girl I met I thought she was
alright
but then it seemed that she was
babyish
so I cut her loose
man she was
good-looking
but childish

> William Rosado
> East Harlem Youth Center

MIXED FEELINGS

I love you like I love food
I love you like I love a roach walking down
                                the street.
You are like the wind that blows from the
                                sea.
You are like a pain in the neck.

Love is like my boyfriend and me.
Love is like the beauty of the world when
                you put it all together.

I love you like I love a dog.
You are like a stinky rat.

> Maribel Bruno
> Julia Richman High School
> New York City

WHEN I WAS CRAZY.....

One day I was over my sister's house,
And I had a cup of coffee,
The coffee tasted weird,
I began to feel strange.
I started to get all hairy and I lost one eye.
I felt like attacking everyone.
I went crazy.
I lost my mind.
About 6 hours later I came out of it.
I knew what had happened.
And I knew it would happen again.

Dorothy Schlesinger
5th Grade
Wharton, New Jersey

MY MOTHER IS PATIENT

I cut class; just walk around the halls,
Yelling the language I use in the streets.

They catch me, send me to the dean;
Call my guardian, and my mother is
        patient.

I go to school, ring the fire alarm;
Get caught, get in trouble,
And my mother is patient.

Walking the streets, I go into a store,
"Cop" something;
Get in trouble, and my mother is patient.

I shoot a guy, then I get shot;
I die;
I'm with my mother, and she is patient.

George Negron
c. Damrosch 1970

WHAT HAVE YOU SEEN LATELY?

I took a picture of lots of birds flying around
around the corner on 121st
I took a picture of some cars
and I took pictures of the
sanitation men working
one of the men had a mask on so none of the dirt
get in his eyes
that's it

I took a picture of the little girl
next door   because Miss Rubin talked about we could
take pictures of   high places   and far away
and I took a picture of her   she was sitting down
and I was upstairs   and I took a picture of her
and then she turned around with her apple   and
she saw me
it snapped her when she turned around
when she turned around she had her apple in her hand
and that's when I snapped her   picture
and she came up   and then she didn't know what was that
machine   so she didn't tell me nothing about that
and then I went up to the roof   and I took a picture of
the bridge   and buildings   all together
and I took a picture of my mother   I think she's
pretty someway
and I took another picture of you know the bridge
because it's sort of like sad   because
it's sort of like foggy
and terrible   and I took a picture of my mother
because she's sort of like   pretty to me
and I like her very much
in a sort of way she's pretty
and I took a picture of the girls next door going to
buy something
with their cart and
and I don't know what else I took a picture of
and all the pictures I took   was for some reason
I had a reason
for taking those pictures   and I can't give you all the
reasons   because there's too many reasons

(from P.S. 96, New York City
with Dick Lourie in the
photography workshop)

25

Collective Novels

Occasionally one encounters a student who is writing a very long story that turns into a novel. But many kids lose heart in the middle of such extensive efforts. Several writers in Teachers & Writers have experimented with class novels.

Poet Clarence Major directed a group of teenagers through a long work which was plotted and written together by passing the manuscript around.

Larry Jenkins, working with a sixth grade class of Chinese and Puerto Rican students with limited English, tried developing a collective novel "sideways." The following is his account of the first class:

We have begun a novel. Its tentative title is "Eddie and Miss Booker: Their Adventures." We began by making up a character. I explained to the class that they were going to write a long book, which would be a combination of everyone's work. The first thing was to invent a leading character. This was done by my going around the room and asking one kid after another questions about the person. This was also done by the "inside" method, first asking about the physical appearance of the character, and then about his likes and dislikes, his personality, is he nice or mean, etc. The character they invented turned out to be something of a monster. His name is Eddie. He is nine feet tall, has green skin, and wears clothes and shoes made out of green paper. He is a mute, is redheaded, and is missing an arm. He is a thief, and although he is married and has a large number of children, he also likes to "get girls". . . . When we had completed the character, we began on his place of residence. They were not nearly so fantastic where this was concerned, as the initial response to "Where does he live?" was a New York apartment at a very specific address. They took off quite soberly from there, giving him a filthy three rooms and orange crate and cardboard furniture. As another character, they invented Miss Booker. This was apparently the name of a real person the kids all knew. It took a while for me to make them understand, and with some I was unsuccessful, that the Miss Booker we were inventing was not necessarily the same as the one they knew. They would keep bringing up the real Miss Booker's characteristics even though opposite ones were already on the blackboard for the character. . . . When they heard that if we each wrote five pages there would be a 150 page book about Eddie and Miss Booker, they got very excited, and asked questions about when it would be published, and how much money they would get for it. I told them I didn't know, but that we had to make it as good as it could be first, and then think about all that.

I put this on the blackboard without a word of explanation. By the time I have the diagram completed the kids have realized that "Home" is like the home or goal of children's games. I then explain the operation of the "game": the players (writers) must go in their imagination to each box and, while there, get something. The rule I wrote down on the board is "Get Something at Every Stop." Once they have the basic notion down, I explain that the box with the ??? in it is a free stop and they can have anything happen there. One boy made his own diagram and put in happenings at each stop. In effect he wrote his own diagram rather than filling out the story from the diagram I gave.

—Dick Gallup

Diagram Stories

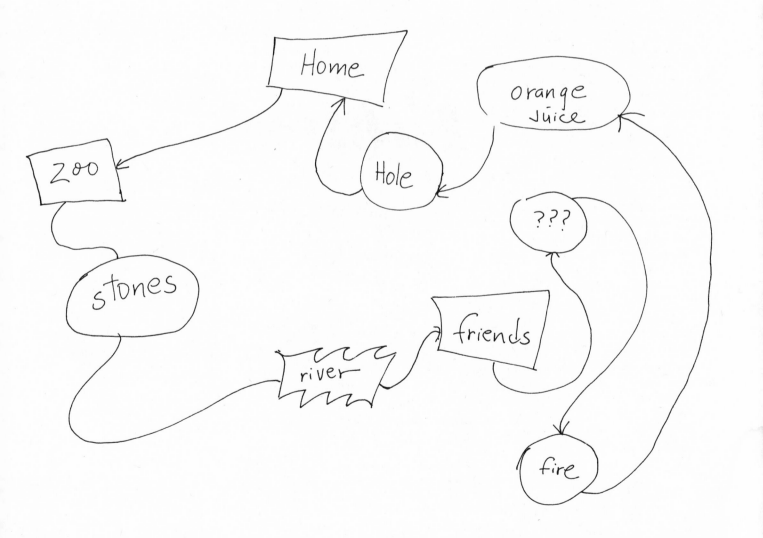

The fable is a form particularly suited for school writing programs. It is short and uses the elements of fairy tales and stories that most children know before they arrive in school. It is not rigid and may embody indirectly (through the use of animal types, ambiguous morals, etc.) every and any attitude towards life. It is as suitable for play as serious statement. . . . The appeal of the fable is the license it gives to talk about the underside of accepted human behavior and circumstances. It doesn't require a panorama of characterers, and the resolution is there, in the necessity of a moral. We also see the fable as a form expansible into others such as the long narrative, satire, dramatic dialogue, allegory.

Here is how Lila Eberman used fable writing in a high school class. She began by putting "All that glitters is not gold" on the board and asking for other examples of proverbs. "They came up with the most common—Don't put all your eggs. . . Don't count your chickens. . . You scratch my back I'll scratch yours. . . etc. One student contributed an original: Do unto others' mothers before others' mothers do unto you. One boy remarked that these sayings weren't always true—for instance, regarding "Counting chickens," he always does his chores for his mother and he figures out beforehand how much money he'll earn and how he is going to spend the money—and he is usually right. I then asked the students to choose a proverb and make up a story to illustrate it."

Fables

Another approach involves using the animal types that appear as characters in many fables. The idea is to talk of the animal expressions in ordinary language (sly as a fox, works like a horse, chicken, bird-brained, scapegoat, blind as a bat, cool cat, monkeying around, stubborn as a mule) and to lead into the use of animal types in written forms to represent certain human types.

There are many other ways to begin. One can talk about the common characters in fables: the trickster, the hustler, the boaster. One can talk about the themes that occur in fables: on not being contented with one's lot, the fate of the boaster, the consequences of lying, the triumph of the clever (or the stupid), etc. Some student fabulists get pleasure out of reversing the traditional morals, as in The Wolf Who Cried Boy. (See examples.)

Herb Kohl & Karen Kennerly

DO UNTO OTHERS
AS OTHERS DO UNTO YOU

One night a boy called Herbert walked through the streets, until all of a sudden the peacefulness of night was broken when he saw a group of about 20 charge at him. He, not knowing what to do, stepped to the side because he thought that maybe they were not after him. But one of the gangsters called out there he is, then Herbert began to run for what seemed to be his life. But to no avail, the gang caught up to him and gave him a beating like never before. The police and the ambulance were called to pick up what was left of him. He was hospitalized for two months. After he came out of the hospital he said he was going to get even, so he bought himself a tonson machinegun. That night he waited where the gang hangs out. Before he knew it the gang appeared coming up the block. Herbert was waiting and ready. As they passed by he came out shooting madly at each and every one of them. None of them survived. The police caught him and arrested him. Soon he was brought to trial. He lost the case. Before his sentence was to be announced the Judge said do you have anything to say.

And Herbert said do unto others as others do unto you.

Irving Lopez
10th Grade
Benjamin Franklin High School
New York City

One day an ostrich named Johnny wondered why he did not fall off the earth and when he went to bed he knew that he was off his feet so he would tie himself to the bedpole at night. One night when Johnny went to sleep he saw a vision of an angel named Leonard, and the angel told Johnny that there was nothing to fear and that an angel named gravity was holding you down. And from that time on Johnny never feared anything again.

Nothing in life is to be feared, it is only to be understood.

Leonard Gumbs
10th Grade
Benjamin Franklin High School
New York City

In 2071 the pollution will be deep as snow, deep
       as Wilt Chamberlain, deep as the middle of the ocean.
In 2071 the spaceman will be in space without
       oxygen holding his breath
King Kong will go to Hong Kong to play Ping Pong.
Godzilla will burn the world
And King Kong will play baseball with Pluto.
In 2071 the buildings will look like crackerjacks
      and people will be eating them
The houses will look like Hostess cupcakes
There will be cloud buildings
People will go around with flying cars on Continental
      trailways
And will have camp on the moon
In 2071 the people will eat mice and rats
The dinosaurs will come back to life and rule the earth.

Grade 4
Horace Mann School
Bayonne, New Jersey

Creating Worlds

by Marvin Hoffman

Teachers & Writers began working on an imaginary worlds project out of a desire to find issues of sufficient breadth and interest to allow for sustained independent writing by students. (See *Imaginary Worlds* published by Teachers & Writers, summer 1971, revised edition, fall 1974.) We were displeased with the fragmentary, disjointed quality of much that had emerged from the program where the work from week to week often did not seem to build on itself. In addition we were looking for ways to relate writing to the other aspects of the school curriculum. Utopias seemed a natural point of juncture between writing, social studies, geography and almost any other school subject, depending on the interests of the teacher.

To begin with, the utopian idea was broken down into a number of seemingly manageable subject areas which students could deal with in weekly sections. These areas included:

    traveling to the imaginary world
    religion
    schools
    raising children
    war
    work

Obviously the list can expand out in any direction that suits the interests of the students and the teacher. For example, one teacher who was very interested in meteorology had her students working on descriptions of life in imaginary worlds with unusual climates—a land where it snowed all the time, a land of constant heat, etc. It becomes less necessary as the project progresses to provide weekly subject areas for students to work on. A list of possible areas should suffice to carry them through their own independent work. But at the outset, at least, the various subjects were introduced by reading quotes from the vast literature of utopias and dystopias (nightmare worlds)—books like H. G. Wells' *The Time Machine, Brave New World, 1984, Slaughterhouse-Five* by Kurt Vonnegut, and the *Collected Works of*

Henri Michaux. The list of utopian fictions is almost endless, but a selected bibliography is included at the end of *Imaginary Worlds*.

Even the best of ideas wears thin after a while and the teacher must be able to detect the signs of boredom when they set in. For most of the classes which were working on the utopias project this point came after about seven or eight sessions. In one class where the teacher had hit on the idea of treating each subject in the form of a letter from the traveler to his family or friends describing some aspect of his experiences in this new world, the class stopped writing after seven sessions and began editing and illustrating what they had done, ironing out inconsistencies, filling in missing details. What emerged was a class library of utopian "novels."

Two other long projects which emerged from the utopian writing were a long play about an imaginary land and the writing of a geography book filled with facts about an imaginary country—terrain, natural resources, industries, climate, etc. This was also a grand opportunity for students to satirize textbooks.

NOWHERE LAND

Nowhere land was founded in the year nothing-0.
The person who founded it was Sir No-Where.
When Sir No-Where got there he saw something,
But it was nothing.
Sir No-Where brought me there,
But I found myself nowhere.
Nowhere Land is beautiful.
Their transportation is riding or walking in air.
Their occupation is making chicken in the basket,
And eating it in the casket.

> Patricia McKnight
> Grade 5

Here are some other activities that other writers have tried. They can stand by themselves or be integrated into a larger project.

BESTIARIES

A bestiary is a collection of imaginary animals, the best example of which is Borges' classic *The Book of Imaginary Beings* (Avon, paper). The task is to create new species of animals, describe their physical characteristics, their habitat, their eating habits, and other unusual qualities—and if possible, to illustrate it.

The Alorse is like a horse made of the alphabet. It walks very stiffly. It comes from a city called Esrola in a place called Allor. Allor is down 2500 miles in the center of the earth. Alorses are made in factories. Then they come up a long tube into a house in Oklahoma. The house is at 420 Cautauqua St. in Norman, Oklahoma. Then they are shipped around the world. The Alorse collects humans, usually girls, but it will take a boy if necessary. When it gets hungry it eats iron. That is why they don't have iron poor blood. If you see one, run. He will capture you if you don't and how would you like to be part of his collection?

> Jamie Callan
> 4th Grade, New York City

CREATION AND APOCALYPSE STORIES

Here is a kind of mythmaking in which students are encouraged to write their own accounts of how the world was created or destroyed. Readings from a good collection of creation epics from differing cultures would be a good source.

HOW THE _____ GOT HIS _____

The most inspired collection of this kind of tale is Rudyard Kipling's *Just So Stories* (Airmont Publishing Co., 22 East 60 St., N.Y., N.Y. 10021; 60¢) which includes "How the Camel Got His Hump," "How the Rhinoceros Got His Skin," and "How the Alphabet Was Made." Another delightful book is Julius Lester's collection *Black Folktales* (Richard W. Baron). The students will take it from there.

MAGIC GUNS

If the world were different, ordinary objects would function differently. If there were no wars, then guns would magically perform different functions.

This is a banana shooter and apple shooter. Nobody in this world has seen this kind of gun. I am going to show you how it shoots. You see all those buttons: you press them, then you press the trigger. And it shoots out bananas and apples. Today Miss Glotzer came late. She told our X teacher, I am going to grab a bite. I said stop, I have a gun that shoots apples and bananas. 5¢ for 5 bananas. She said thanks. I said always at your service.

> Gilbert the pro
> 4th Grade, New York City

The visual and writing possibilities are boundless. (See *Absolutely Mad Inventions*, Bibliography p. 68.)

Spoofs and Parodies

Children (especially from the ages of 8 to 12) are usually possessed by an outrageously healthy sense of parody—they mock their teachers, the media, their classmates and their schoolwork.

They are seeing, perhaps for the first time in their lives, a lot of how the world is, and out of their feelings of powerlessness in a world of adults, they impersonate characters and create jokes that make themselves laugh, feel better and feel smarter.

When children learn that they can entertain themselves, that they don't have to depend on TV or adults for amusement, they begin to practice their sense of humor—to make themselves laugh. Unfortunately, they can't change many of the absurdities they see, but at least their mockery and laughter can be a true expression of their feelings and insights.

If they frequently drive adults up the wall with their Froggy-the-Gremlin mimicry and the constant infusion of cartoon figures and TV plots into their writing, it's important to consider that children not only copy but reweave their media heroes into personal myths. The Beatles or Nixon and the Road Runner, among others, become the larger-than-life stuff of their imaginations, the mythological figures who embody their hopes and hates.

"Sometimes I look at life in the fun mirror at a carnival. I see myself as a profound, incisive wit, concerned with man's inhumanity to man. Then I stroll to the next mirror and I see a pompous subjective ass whose humor is hardly spiritual."

—Lenny Bruce

Who can take this world or himself seriously all the time? Who in his life in these United States hasn't attempted a couple of movie-star imitations, vamped upon the inanities of TV commercials, or caricatured the personality of a popular politician? These popular parodies, cultural jokes on the style of our national life, help protect us from becoming caricatures of ourselves. And they can help make us feel a lot better about people and situations that we often can't do much about.

REWRITING CONVENTIONAL READERS

Eric Mann describes this experience of working with Herb Kohl in Newark:

"Herb began the lesson by showing the class the cover of a new book he had written. The book cover was a photograph of wall graffiti. He asked the students if they thought such a book would be used in the public schools, and the students dutifully replied that it wouldn't be because it was 'too cool.' Herb asked, 'If they won't use a book like this, what kinds of books will they use?' Willie and Tiny said simultaneously, 'Dick and Jane' with a tone of voice that expressed both genuine distaste and a desire to please Herb and me.

"Herb was really turned on, dropped whatever plans he originally had for the lesson, and said, 'OK. If you don't like Dick and Jane let's write our own Dick and Jane.' His enthusiasm was contagious. The sentences came forth quickly."

MENUS

Disgusting or otherwise. Hairball soup, grilled baboon legs stuffed with garbage, chocolate skeleton juice.

Ask for a menu fit for an enemy. Few kids will resist giving you one.

CRAZY MATH

Concoct your own math problems by substituting words for numbers.

1 man + 1 woman =
         something interesting.

Jackie Gleason - 100 lbs. =
         Mission Impossible.

Or crazy math problems in story form, of the "two-trains-leave-Chicago-at-the-same-time" variety.

QUIZZES

I.Q. Tests, Multiple Choice, Idiot Quizzes. The only immediate answer to the battery of testing in all schools. Write impossibly difficult or strange questions.

NEWSPAPER PARODIES

Ripley's Believe It Or Not
Dear Abby
Gossip Column
Drunken (or Crazy) Newscast
Interview With Famous Personality
Weather Report
Fashions

These can be done separately or in conjunction with the composing of a peculiar newspaper. For instance, read a typical fashion show piece and have the kids parody or exaggerate it with their own reportage of imaginary fashions.

IMAGINARY FAMILY TREES

An invitation to concoct whole histories full of skullduggery, with a skeleton in every closet; or star-crossed lovers; rags-to-riches careers; family curses. Can be done with or without a diagram of the tree itself.

POLEMICS

Have the kids select a controversial topic, such as Prejudice/Brotherhood, and have them write two essays—one attacking the position, the other defending it. ("Air pollution is bad for your health," etc., vs. "Air pollution makes the air dark, so my mother thinks it's still night and I don't have to go to school.") This is the beginning of irony.

—Ron Padgett

ADVERTISEMENTS

Kids make up their own products and write advertising copy for them, or they can write versions of ads already in existence. E.g., "What a wonderful time for the terrible taste of Kent!"

Or they can write about how our lives are curiously affected by an ad-infested society.

I am a chaise lounge chair
and here she comes again
with her Lord & Taylor shorts
and Charles of the Ritz fingernails
and Clairol Number 27 ash hair
a weight watchers reject
she plunges upon my proud yellow seat
and pushes me back
and sweats
shouting orders to her husband.
He hurries out of the house
Everyone crowds around her
she sets a cool glass of Metrecal
on my arm.
and picks up her copy of Cosmopolitan
I groan beneath the weight of her
The hot sun beats down upon this freak of femininity
Who sits content in my lap.
I am a chaise lounge chair.

> *Beth Schenerman*
> *Bergen, New Jersey*

AD

a teacher for sale he cost a penney his
name is Mr. Meth is chip buy him before
is to late buy him He look like a horse
You could use him as a horse

> *a 9th grade non-reader*

OUR DICK AND JANE

This is Dick.
What kind of Dick?
A boy named Dick.

This is Jane.
What kind of Jane?
A Mary Jane. Boy do they taste good and last long.

I wonder where they live.
They live in a cardboard box on Washington Street.

I didn't know they could afford a TV.

Dick was playing with matches and the house caught on fire.
Somebody call the fire department quick before Mary Jane melts.
"You bad boy, I told you not to play with matches," said Jane.
He said, "Aw shut up, you aren't my mother. We better get out quick or else I'll burn and you'll melt."
Dick jumped out the window and Jane melted into peanut butter.

SCIENTIFIC LECTURE: ON HAIR

It's a little known factor that hair comes from the brain. Your hair comes up through your scalp by being pushed up by blood cells. The color of your hair is the color of your brain. Hair is really the part of your brain that isn't very smart. It is pushed out of your head because it has no use in the brain and it just clutters up the space your brain has for knowledge.

It is also a little known factor that hair is really alive. Hair has to go to school to learn how to go through your scalp. They also go to school to learn to protect themselves from dandruff. People with dandruff have very illiterate hair. But do not necessarily have illiterate minds. In school they also have gym period. When a lot of them are playing in school and pounding on the ground it is commonly known as a headache. The hair that invented the headache was Alan B. Excedrin. Bad headaches are named after him and are Excedrin headaches. In school they also learn how to numb themselves when being cut at the barbers.

When hair sleeps it sleeps straight up. When you get up before your hair does, it (your hair) stands straight and water or a comb and brush will wake it up and this makes it lay on your scalp.

Hairs need lots of psychoanalysts because there are so many of them crowded into one place that a lot of them have an inferiority complex and they also have (some of them) a feeling of difference from others if they are the only gray in a head of browns. Some of them are prejudiced because sometimes there are about five black hairs in a bunch of grayish-white hair and the grayish-white push the hairs to the bottom of the scalp.

As I discussed earlier blood cells push up part of your brain to form hair. Bald people have weak blood cells for an obvious reason.

As some people have noticed, hair doesn't grow only on heads. This is because some people do have little bits of brain in the rest of your body. People with hair on their chests have smart chests. Women have very stupid chests. The reason that more grows on the top part of your body is because it is nearer your brain. Women have more hair on their heads (most of the time) than men because their brain stays in their head, mostly because their extra rib holds their brain in the head by bouncing it back all the way up.

When people dye their hair and then cut it, your hair might grow back either way, because the brain might get used to the dyed color.

It is rumored that hair has developed a way to make itself indestructible. It will then grow forever and it will drown the part of your brain with the knowledge and will take over the earth with the worms (discussed in a previous lecture).

Michael Olenick
9th Grade

A car is 495 tons. It goes 64 M.P.H. A boy was 1/8 inch from the road. In how much time will it take for him to eat his sandwich?

Answer _____

If Bill had 1 stick of gum he chewed for 3 seconds, how much does he have left?

Answer _____

by Alicia & Melody
5th Grade
P.S. 20, New York City

I Know You; You're the Poet

by Phillip Lopate

WHERE WILL I PUT MYSELF?

I walk into a strange classroom and there is cheering and applause. I've done nothing to earn this popularity but I like it. Three kids come rushing up to grab my arms: "I know you, you're the poet." Later I realize that I am being watched carefully by the girls washing the sink in the back, by the various in and out groups, to see whom I will favor: the three kids, the blacks, the whites, the show-offs, the slow learners. One mistake and they will decide I am "unfair." Right now I am riding a wave of good will granted me because I look a little weird and I'm a novelty. Something called a Poet—which I have to keep reminding myself I really am! Where does a poet stand in a child's eyes? Not as high as the athlete, but above the teacher.

And now the teacher comes forward to ask the class to give me their undivided attention. I wonder where I will locate myself: by her desk, in front of the blackboard, or somewhere completely unexpected. All these desks, these angles of vision, the stage feels wrong. Not my space. And it is the beginning of a year-long struggle to build a comfortable space for myself in the classroom, which will also give itself to creative writing.

I tell them a bit about myself. My background, why I'm here—sounding as casual as possible. I'm conscious of being too tall; I want to bend in half to be at their level. I start inclining my head ostrich-like in front of the blackboard. I move around a lot. Maybe I read them a poem. I sense their detachment; where is all this leading to? A little side-conversation ... I'm already losing some of my stardust! Then I pull it all together, WHAMO, and before they know it we're into the Idea I had up my sleeve, and paper is being handed out and there are choices on the board. I tell myself I want to get a sighting on their interests and their talents, but I'm also thinking "They better write the first day or they will goldbrick forever after."

So the kids begin to learn the bitter truth, that this poet is merely another in a long series of taskmasters.

All the papers are read aloud. I collect them next week. The teacher assures me it went well. "Usually they're much more distracted. And they liked you." I'm not so sure. I know they liked me before I opened my mouth; then I became just another adult rapping to them. But I'm delighted I survived.

TAKING DICTATION

Three weeks pass. Some kids still hate to write. I feel foolish ordering them: Write! Did I ever write a single poem because someone stood over me and told me to? What am I, a floor manager? Yet the unspoken pressure is to leave with a fat sheaf of papers, if not to impress the teacher, then my boss or the State Arts Council that is paying my salary or the other poet-teachers who are in subtle competition for who can midwife the most child masterpieces.

I learn to say, "You don't have to write anything," and to hope that before the term is over the turned off ones will come around. But occasionally you can sense that a child would like to write and is just too frightened. The genius of teaching is knowing when a person is ready to open or to close. I sit down and start talking with him. When his thoughts have sufficiently congealed I start taking dictation. The miracle: he sees that his thoughts have a form and can be turned instantly into writing. Now he's intrigued. He would like to keep me around and have me follow him all day as a scribe to record his musing. It is hard to say which is more important: the discovery that he has something in his mind worth preserving as writing, or the sustained attention of an adult.

By this time a small crowd is pushing round us, each demanding the same service for himself and wondering, What's so special about Freddy. All have grasped in a second the advantages of this new technique, Dictation, as a liberation from the tedium of compositions. Me, I'm feeling cornered, thrown into the lagoon with the piranha fish.

"One at a time. . ."

And if you've brought a typewriter the crush is even greater, because the novelty of machines is irresistible. You must hold them back from hitting the keys over and under your shoulder.

When the class is working at its best, with production 40% up and most students busy on their own pieces or collaborating in small groups, I can wander over to the kids who are "out of it," the misfits. Here is where dictation makes most sense. It encourages that physical closeness which is so important, the two of us bending over the same paper, starting to trust each other.

I can't describe the tenderness of some of these collaborations. Once a first grader dictated with perfect assurance a beautiful poem about God's love, and I felt as if I were present at a miracle. Another time I asked an older boy, who seemed unhappy, to start talking to himself as if he were alone. He dictated, title and all, "The Sadness."

GOD'S STORY OF LOVE

God is everything
He plays with the clouds
We're his marionettes
If he ever wanted to very much
He'd make us fly
Whatever we do he makes us do
With his fingers
If we sell Kool Aid
He makes our mothers get out the
    pot and make the Kool Aid.
He makes the ball fly
And he makes it bounce.

Jonathan Frisch
Twin Pine Day School
Oakland, California

THE SADNESS

Helping my father wash the car
He tells me to get the water
Marvin turn on the hose pipe.
    Turn on the hose.
It's on.
All right that's good. Bring it here.
Now we splash the soap on
Marvin run the water on the car
All right that's good. Turn it off.
Now let's dry the car off
Gotta give me some money to go get a soda
Marvin you don't have to help me no more
Here's $5.
I go over to the wall.
Then I start staring.
I look down the street
I look up the street
What do I see?
I see one man coming with a carriage carrying junk
And a freight train running on its lane
There's no kids my size
Anyhow I'm outside
So I guess I'll talk to myself
Well I wish I had a horse
I look down the street and here come a mule.
They start clearing the junk house
So the mule can come and dump his load

I wish I had a darn horse.
I always wanted a horse and Dad know it
But I had to stop being afraid of horses first
Someone said they'll kick you to death
Mom and Dad say when we go down South
We'll get a horse.
And Dad say he'll get him one and me one too
So what am I worrying about
I'll be glad when I go down South
It is so warm there

Marvin
P.S. 75
New York City

Yet for all these epiphanies I have never lost an uneasy, guilty feeling about taking dictation. How much am I shaping the work through arranging the words in lines? How much has been censored by his awareness of my smile and frowns while recording? What about the words I don't take down? Am I helping him to become his own editor? Wouldn't it be as useful for him to struggle through a written piece that came completely from himself? Will he become dependent on me?

After the second dictation from the same person I tell him next time he can write it himself. He seems skeptical he can do it. "But it's not as much fun!" he insists. And it isn't. During the next few sessions his eyes follow me with a hangdog look as if I had betrayed his trust. He understands the trick—the same thing his other teachers pulled. It's this universal aberration of the adults, the idée fixe, to get him to read and write. It's not enough apparently that we've opened the way for him to express himself verbally. So the duel of wills goes on: I give in and take dictation a few more times. He gives in a little and writes me something. For the rest of the year we are bound to each other, happy to meet in the halls, tentative, shy, like people who have become intimate too quickly.

DO IT FOR ME

Every week I present a new writing idea. The kids have come to expect it. I talk to friends who are also teaching, I consult the manuals of creative writing, I buy materials, I hang around libraries, I compile shopping lists. A period of great fermentation. Everything is turning into a writing assignment in my head. I am appalled to realize that the number of creative writing assignments is as infinite as things in the world. The night before going into class I try to convince myself that one idea shines above the rest. I believe in it; I go to sleep; in the morning six other assignments seem equally possible. I am riding the bus to school thinking A, B, C, D, or E? Or M? Suddenly I decide it has to be G, G, G...!

I am still walking to the front of the class mumbling to myself: A, B, C, G...

"Now class, I want you to give Phillip your undivided attention."

Who hasn't been struck, on uttering the words "Today I thought we might write about...", with the total unreality of his proposition. Why snowflakes and not carrots? Why satire and not tragedy? Everything comes equally from left field. And in that split second between the introduction and the telling of what it is the class will have to do, who hasn't—staring down at 30 pairs of child-eyes, ready to inform him if he has struck pay dirt or banged his thumb—gone dizzy, wished he could hold off the judgment a little longer, and fallen into the abyss between the two halves of his sentence?

If only I could follow a Curriculum! Some master plan to execute unswervingly from week to week. I see them only once a week, and the task of drawing a continuity between the assignments keeps getting harder. And when I try to follow up a successful start, often it seems that too much has intervened in their lives and the idea already feels stale to them. I try to force some continuity, but it's mostly for my own conscience. In the end I tell myself that they are getting a rounded writing experience from all this variety. Maybe they are. We have had some fabulous successes along the way, which memories keep us going. Nevertheless, *the arbitrariness of my assignments* continues to nag at me.

One day I try an assignment that falls utterly flat. No relevance to anyone's imagination anywhere. Then I am surprised and moved as certain kids diligently carry it out, not because they're afraid of me but because we've been through a lot and they decide to humor me. They do it almost out of a desire to make me feel better—with that kindness and childish tact that's very mysterious. I begin to realize I am banking on their love. Behind all the ideas and creative motivators is the unspoken appeal: "Do it for me."

CHILDREN WITHOUT TEACHERS

I have the urge to know: what do the kids talk about when adults aren't around? What would they write like if not asked to write, but merely for their own amusement? The record of "un-colonized" children's literature seems to me a dark area. First children were taught how to write pious holiday and nature verse. Now the kiddie anthologies stress the poignant, the social-conscious, or even the avant-garde, but the hand of the anthologist and poet-teacher is very apparent. Anyone familiar with the contemporary literary scene knows that Kenneth Koch's delightful students' work has more than a casual resemblance to Koch's delightful verse, that David Henderson's students write more or less like David Henderson, Ron Padgett's kids like Ron Padgett, David Shapiro's students' poems read like David Shapiro's, and my students' rather like mine. Some of this influence is inevitable and even desirable. What else should a poet teach but himself? And no matter how you may try to be neutral your prejudices will shine through; the kids are masters at reading just such cues.

In the Renaissance a young painter was apprenticed to Jacopo Bellini with the understanding that he would learn first to paint Bellinis. Perhaps what makes the question more ethically disturbing here is that kids don't know what they're signing up for. It's alarming to think of a whole generation of schoolkids learning to parrot the mannerisms of contemporary writing and to produce works that look, to us, intriguingly modern without their really understanding what they are doing.

Again and again I wonder how they would write without us. I intercept messages passed under the desk just to read them for style! I peek at the graffiti in kids' notebooks. And I begin to form hunches about children's culture. It is satiric and at the same time heroic, it moves uncannily toward forbidden subjects, it is euphonious and violent.

THE EAVESDROPPER

In the background Sherry is whispering to Gail that she will "get her" after school. Maria is secretly lifting the petticoat of her doll under the desk. Robert is sulking because the other kids only want him around for his toy guns. More and more I am becoming distracted by, or tuned into, the private chorus of disorders and early sorrows which mocks the pretense of orderly classroom learning.

Today the whole class seems strangely dispirited, grumpy. What's the matter? A trip has been canceled. Can I ignore the mood and launch into the surefire writing idea I had brought, hoping my enthusiasm will take them out of themselves? Somehow I feel it would be a disaster. So we talk about the canceled trip, then about disappointments and remembered hurts. While we're listening to each other something triggers off another, more meditative, writing idea I had been storing for future use.

Sensing the mood. This becomes my motto if not always my practice. First you study all the creative writing formulas, yes, because kids appreciate games and structures. Then you file them away until the right moment arrives to introduce them. It comes down to developing in myself that elusive intuition of group feeling without which all the writing ideas in the world will fall lifeless. To know how to use the energy that's already there: when to move with the grain, when it's more instructive to turn against it.

This is I think what George Dennison means when he says you throw out the curriculum and make your course of study "the lives of children."

Rather than always second-guessing the kids' interests I begin asking them directly for subjects. But when I demand of a large class point-blank: "What would you like to write about?" it usually provokes anxiety, trivia, insincerity and discouragement. So I eavesdrop on the small talk of the students entering the room, and many times I throw away my lesson plans and go with something that's in the air. Once the second-graders came running into class shouting some scandal about vomit, in the hopes of starting an uproar, and I got them to write a pretty good vomit poem. This brand of opportunism requires quick reflexes and a strong stomach.

I also take to hanging around the schoolyard and the lunchroom, fooling with the kids without trying to get anything out of them. In short I let myself be a human being instead of merely a writing teacher. If at first I see myself as a patient anthropologist gathering clues on the culture of children, in the end all this kidding around is what sweetens the job, and stays with me.

A RATIONAL WORK FLOW

Everything is beginning to jell. Now that I am beginning to know the kids I can suggest individual projects: two to make a comic book because that's what they love, another to finish her saga of the girl who fell in love with her horse. The class separates naturally into individuals and affinity groups. It resembles a clubhouse more than a mass rally. I understand now that the assignments, aside from what they taught, were a necessary pretext, a smokescreen for us to get to know each other while doing something together.

When the energy begins to sag again, we do a play. Dramatics can unify a class as nothing else. I am amazed at the tone of serious work: division of labor sets in, students sort themselves into work groups, even get each other to keep quiet. Later on in the year a class magazine becomes the spur for new writing. Stories start appearing from nowhere and they are unadulterated products of children's writing. By now I just circle around, throwing things into the stew, checking the flame, hovering.

My dream for the class is coming true: a rational work flow. . .

In the meantime there have been a lot of slack and untidy moments that didn't always look right to officials sticking their heads in the door. In fact it was more like bedlam. So I pray indulgence to the powers that be for all teachers to have the time and the privilege I was given as a specialist to make my messy mistakes. ■

These exercises are intended to encourage children to be adventurous and inquisitive about language. By emphasizing the pure play of words, they can help children create writing which pushes against the borders of common sense with strange combinations and surprises. The writer of dull essays or stories may startle his teacher (and himself) with a Lewis Carroll-like ear by following one of these structures. If these exercises end up occasionally in what seems to be encouragement of nonsense for its own sake, they can also lead quite naturally into investigations of grammar and curiosity about the origins of language.

Language Games

ACROSTICS

Poems based on names. Write your own (or someone else's) name vertically and then use each letter as the first letter of the first word in its line (see examples).

ALLITERATIVE POEMS

Each line has many words beginning with the same letter. E.g., "The brave bumblebee bounced off the black Buick." The poem could continue with all b's or using different letters in each line.

CUBIST POEMS

The term "Cubist" is used very loosely here. Ask the kids for a letter of the alphabet. Suppose someone says D. What word for D? Dumbbell, they might say. Then get another letter, X. What word? Express. So the title of the poem is DUMBBELL EXPRESS. Continue like this until the poem ends. (If you don't know when the poem should end, ask the children.) Another way, if you're doing this at the typewriter with a bunch of kids, is to use the order of the top row of keys for your first letters, with the kids supplying the words.

LIST OF WORDS

Write a list of words on the board; try to make an interesting and colorful combination. One writer chose: bulldog, headache, lamp-shade, polevault, concept, baloney, Alabama, planet, wiggle, and, running, however, angel, iceberg, filing cabinet. Lists may be longer or shorter. Have the kids weave as many of these words as possible into a poem or story.

DEFINITIONS

Write a list of words which you can reasonably expect your students don't know—interesting sounding or looking words such as stylized, noxious, solenoid, pretentious, circumlocution, syzygy, mantissa, punctilious, vacillation, zephyr, etc. Have the kids write (without use of a dictionary), what they think the words might mean.

MISTRANSLATIONS

I took Tommy aside and had him do a mistranslation. It struck me that working from a strict text would get around the problem of his having "no ideas."

I explained that I knew he didn't know French; the idea was to repeat the sounds aloud or simply to look at the words and follow whatever ideas come into his head.

He knew instinctively what to do but proceeded very slowly as if feeling his way along a dark tunnel. There was a look of excitement in his eyes, but fear also, and he turned to me often not so much for suggestions (which I tried not to give) as for confirmation in this scary unfolding of a poem.

He said how strange it was that you could take words in a foreign language and translate them without understanding. I think it had some of the mystery of alchemy for him. At every line he thought of and discarded several options, and after the first two lines he strove for a continuity between lines; that is, he wanted the whole thing to read like a story, however 'nonsensical' it seemed to be coming out.

—Phillip Lopate

CODES

This is an interest easy to tap, since codes are already part of the underground communications system of school children. Scholastic's paperbacks, *How to Write and Send Secret Messages*, and *Codes and Ciphers* make easy-to-follow suggestions of classic codes. Most of the codes are fairly inevitable and kids enjoy stumbling on them by themselves.

One possibility is to write a poem or story using certain words which are code for other words (or cryptograms, using certain letters as code for certain other letters). To begin, make a list of words and what their code words are. Then substitute. E.g., if cucumber is code for nose: "He blew his cucumber."

CROSSWORD PUZZLES

Kids can make their own crosswords and exchange them with each other. A variation is to spell out whole phrases or titles (try books, movies, TV shows, proverbs, etc.) in crossword puzzle form and give hints in whole phrases too.

WORD RUMMY

This is a game whose rules are adaptable to differing situations. Essentially the game consists of using vocabulary flash cards or drawing your own word cards and trying to make sentences or ideas out of them. The results can be intriguingly compressed, as in these examples from 4th-graders:

two cat feet make very
warm ball together

rain door
girl's pig face

children
grow
ask
them

Longer pieces can be developed by not confining oneself to the word cards alone, but writing a sentence around each word turned over.

(Acrostic Poems)

Most marvelous music maker
At all times
Though
The
Horrible
Eky
Water falls on the piano.

Matthew has
A
Nice
Diddle-
Ee-do
Life
Because he has
A
"U"
In his
Marvelous name.

Matthew Mandelbaum
5th Grade
P.S. 75, New York City

YANKEE DRINKER

Labor is hard work
In the grape fields
Nacer drank too much and got drunk and
Died. We were
Sad. We found out the grapes were poisoned
And that Nacer did it to kill himself. He was a Yankee.
Yankee go home.

Lindsay Dixon
6th Grade
Oakland, California

HOW TO MAKE A RAINBOW

Get balloons of all colors.
Throw about 4 or 5 buckets of water in a jar.
Shake it up.
Set it down for at least one year.
Then throw it up in the air.
It will spread out.

Joan Helmer

SENTENCE EXPANSIONS and CONTRACTIONS

This and the other two games described on this page are half-quoted, half-paraphrased from an article by Tony Kallet, "Fun and Games with the English Language" (*Outlook*, pub. Mountain View Center for Environmental Education, Univ. of Colorado, Boulder 80302). The games are difficult, but useful.

Begin with any sentence. Expand or contract that sentence by replacing words at the rate of, say, two words for every one. Thus "The dog ran quickly" could become "The pink tiger ran quickly;" and then "The pink tiger ate pancakes quickly" and so on until every word has been replaced by two. Here's a sample contraction from Kallet's article, which kidnaps words and sense in two's.

Six sad sheep sat
    silently mourning
       the midnight moon.

Slippery sheep sat
    silently mourning
       the midnight moon.

Slippery sheep sat
    silently mourning
       the dawn.

Rupert sat silently
      mourning the dawn.

Stop mourning the dawn.

Behold the dawn!

Behold Jello!

Oops!

SUBSTITUTIONS

For any word in a sentence, anything may be substituted as long as the "sentenceness" is kept inviolate; i. e., as long as the parts of speech stay the same through the word changes. This is a good way to show how syntactical form is constant, no matter how the content changes. You can even use made-up words, as in "Twas brillig and the slithy toves" from *Alice in Wonderland.*

—Kallet

ARRANGING WORDS

Especially useful in suggesting some of the features of words which determine their positions in sentences. Write down a fairly straightforward sentence (no capital letters), cut it up into individual words, tell the player that there are six words, say, and give him one word. Ask him to write down what he thinks your sentence is. Give him a second and ask him to place it where he thinks it goes in relation to the first word. Give him all the words one at a time, having him revise his sentence as he goes. What he comes up with may make no sense at all, though he will have made it correct, grammatically. Or he might have a plausible sentence, but not yours. Or he might have yours.

—Kallet

NEW LANGUAGES

Among the most interesting codes are the ones wherein a symbol is substituted for a letter (*=A, #=B). Taking this a step or two further, one can substitute symbols or pictures for whole words, like the Oriental "ideogram" that encompasses whole objects, concepts, images in a single symbol.

James Herndon had a discussion of the creation of a new written language in *How To Survive In Your Native Land* (Simon and Schuster).

"They wrote down lists of common words and when we had the lists we'd start making a picture or symbol to stand for it. . . . Then we'd choose the best symbol and make lists of those and after we had a couple of hundred or so we'd start translating simple fairy tales into our new language, or making up stories to write in it, and put the stories on huge decorated pieces of paper and send them over to Frank's class to see if they could decipher them. . . . We talked about the necessity of briefer, less complicated forms. . . . We went on and made certain kinds of words different colors when we made posters . . . blue for things, red for actions, green for descriptions, and so on. . . ."

(But read it all and see it in his perspective.)

GIVING DIRECTIONS

Write out the directions for simple tasks—cooking an omelette, tying a shoe, brushing your teeth.

Don't take anything for granted; imagine the reader knows nothing and you must provide perfectly understandable, easy-to-follow directions.

Teach someone how to put on a suit jacket, buy a car, make a speech, fall asleep, walk, scream, laugh. Compose a manual, a how-to book with illustrations.

HALF OF THE POEM IS CRAZY
(Mistranslation)

My gold brown hair and all my
wooden teeth are in the deep sea.
An hour later he blew up, and his
trunk or case fell in his well. I
never had hydrophobia in my house.

My mirror said, no, I must go
when the clock strikes 10 or I'll
be blown up into chain and shatter
my window. Then dye my hair
dark brown. So don't stop me!
When the mirror is broken, I
think I'll faint!

Leonard Altisano
Grade 5

BERTIN'S ADVENTURE
(Mistranslation)

Mr. G. Bertin got hanged.
He was involved picking wild
roses in a land called Densee,
holding his Chawawa, wearing
his trunks, going in Van Kussten
River. Playing his dansanet he
was singing his song, Wassail.

Wassail, Wassail the night commit-
ted suicide. We will sing this to
make you bright, that the children
won't go to bed at night.
Unscattered at night the dead
people lie, chaperoned by sirens
deep in the woods.

Lisa Scala
& Joan Korba
Grade 5

HÄLFTE DES LEBENS

Mit gelben Birnen hänget
Und voll mit wilden Rosen
Das Land in den See,
Ihr holden Schwäne,
Und trunken von Küssen
Tunkt ihr das Haupt
Ins heilignüchterne Wasser.

Weh mir, wo nehm' ich, wenn
Es Winter ist, die Blumen, und wo
Den Sonnenschein
Und Schatten der Erde?
Die Mauern stehn
Sprachlos and kalt, im Winde
Klirren die Fahnen.

(Original German, by Hölderlin)

HALF DAY LEAVE
(Mistranslation)

The General burned his hand,
And all the windmills roared.
The land was called Dense.
He had been helping Haup Schwane,
And a trunk fell on General Kussen's head.
The trunk hit Haup Schevane, too,
They fell in Heilgnuchterne Lake.

We admire General Kussen they would say,
When winter came he died, and all the people cried.
He had been shot by Captain Pot.
The day of his funeral the people all cried,
They had been sad because he had died.

Joey Perkins
Grade 5

THE MIDDLE OF LIFE

With yellow pears and full of wild
roses the land hangs down into
the lake, you lovely swans, and
drunken with kisses you dip your
heads into the holy and sober
water.

Alas, where shall I find, when
winter comes, the flowers, and
where the sunshine and shadows
of earth? The walls loom
speechless and cold, in the wind
weathercocks clatter.

(Just in case you're interested in the real
translation.)

Popular, Oral and Street Lore

The next three assignments are all a bit hokey since there is nothing that can honestly replace the natural energy, the anger or the need to declare an "illegitimate" feeling publicly or to violate the sacred property of others that is the setting for graffiti and much of street literature. We're not convinced that these are the best ways to approach these forms, but we had some fun with them and we include them because these subjects belong to us and our culture and belong in the classroom.

THE DIRTY DOZENS

A city schoolyard game more common than basketball is the Dirty Dozens. Its aim is to make the opponent "blow his cool"—that is, cry, yell or fight, by making funny, insulting, sexual remarks about his family—his mother in particular. Boys get reputations for being good dozens players just as they do for being "bad." (On the street, "bad" has good, even heroic connotations.) Often the dozens rhyme, like this one:

> The way he's talkin' 'bout you is a
>   crying shame
> He says he rather ride your Momma
>   than a choo-choo train!

RANKING

"Ranking" (in some areas "cracking" or "mocking" or "The Snaps") is a different name for a less sexual version of the dozens that has gone beyond the black community. Rankouts transcend mere four-letter words; creativity and imagery are their forte.

They exist as an urban form of uproarious, philosophical coping; they are a form of found poetry that picks at the sores of poverty. They make such a mockery of the victims of unbearable circumstances that no one could take himself very seriously in the face of the barrage. The insults focus on ragged clothing, cramped and broken-down apartments, the scarcity of food. They amount to an urban bestiary, featuring the roach, bug, mouse and rat.

There are conditions to the game: though the remarks are often nasty in their candidness about shared poverty, they are rarely personal. You accuse someone in someone else's family (again, preferably his mother) of an ultimate indignity in the face of some graphic symbol of his shame, and you see it as a situation. It's metaphor-making with a passion:

If the man in front of me didn't have more plaid stamps,
I could have got your mother first.

The walls in your house are so close together
that the mice have to walk single file.

I went to your house and stepped on a lit cigarette and your mother shouted, "Who turned off the power?"

I walked in your house and stepped on a roach and your mother said, "Save the white meat."

I came in your house to eat and your mother put a pea on my plate, and I said is this all. She said don't be greedy.

Your mother wears Buster Brown shoes, busted on the outside, brown on the inside.

*Oh man, there's so much dust in your house
the roaches be playing Lawrence of Arabia.*

*When I asked your Ma for a glass of water she said,
"Wait till the tide comes in."*

GRAFFITI

A cliché, but there are still some interesting ways of exploring the international impulse to write on walls, public toilets, etc. You can simply hang brown paper or an old sheet on a large wall or find a wall (or a floor, for that matter) that can survive chalk or magic marker, and give materials to the kids and stand back. There is likely to be a great burst of energy that leaves little besides names, wry suggestions and peace signs.

If you're after something more original you might try improvising a prison scene, or suggest students are lost in a cave, and the surface is the cave or prison wall. They can decorate the walls with what they dream of doing if they ever get out, or what their life is like inside. Drawing on the walls can start them off, or take its place among the writings.

Lila Eberman gave for homework an assignment to copy down everything the students saw written on walls, sidewalks, subway posters, on their way home from school that day. Both classes responded by laughing: "Everything?" "You don't mind foul words?" "There's a lot of poets on my block!" "Your mind's goin' to conk out!"

The next day, according to Lila, "We discussed the reasons that people write on walls, the general conclusion being that the writers wanted to reach a wide audience. We made a frequency chart describing the subject matter of the reading: Love messages (real and puppy love)/ insults (to the reader and others)/ bragging/humor/politics/foul language/ identification of territory/sex/hatred/the truth about people."

Another writer, Anne Sexton, found this way of taking graffiti one step further: "I suggested to Bob Clawson that day after our graffitiblackboard what a great short story it would make: the Graffiti Man—all his experiences; the hidden man publicly declares himself in johns and in tunnels—a rather Dostoevskyan character you could make out of him. . . ."

BLUES AND BLUELETS

The Blues are a great source for poetry, a poetry of intense, direct feelings. The best blues don't waste words. Much of popular music, movies and TV portrays the most vague and romanticized versions of love and suffering—at times, we need music like the blues to say those emotions explicitly, to confront our deepest feelings.

If you're using contemporary rock music as a source of poetry, or a stimulus to writing with teenagers, mix in some timeless blues—records by Blind Lemon Jefferson, Billie Holliday, Bessie Smith, B.B. King, Albert King, Sonny Boy Williamson and Sonny Terry and Brownee McGee. Two of the best books on the blues are Samuel Charters' *The Poetry of the Blues* (Oak Publications) and Leroi Jones' *Blues People*.

Art Berger: "I developed a simple form for a mini-blues—three lines with a 4-4-6 beat called a **bluelet** and a four-liner with a 6-4-4-4 beat called a **rocku**. Using words with a jazz sound and a basic blues beat I asked the class to write their own personal message in this form."

BALLADS AND TALL TALES

For those who wish to explore narrative story-telling in verse or in endless, preposterous tales and gigantic lies.

One class collected street games on a tape recorder, rhymes from their own playgrounds, and then wrote new versions and new rhymes, finally putting old and new together in a book.

BOARD GAMES

Children can make quite ingenious board games of their own (witness the extraordinarily complex football and baseball substitutes that boys create out of school).

Given a hunk of cardboard or a large piece of paper they can design a board and rules. These can grow out of anything the student or class has been doing.

One girl, after a discussion of superstitions, devised a Monopoly-type game in which a roll of the dice got you to squares with instructions like YOU HAVE JUST SEEN A BLACK CAT. GO BACK 6 SPACES, and corresponding good-luck symbols.

Another did a pollution game in which the unlucky dice-thrower kept coming up against exhaust-belching smokestacks and piles of beer cans in search of a clear river!

In the absence of dice, the kids can create another system of throws (a good challenge).

—Rosellen Brown

RIDDLES AND JOKES

Some people who won't write anything else will write riddles and jokes. Try various kinds of riddles and conundrums and hand them around the class to be solved. Make a riddle box for collecting good examples.

The advantage of working with many of these classic poetic structures is that they teach a sense of poetic form based on something other than rhyme; they focus instead on the verse line, the syllable, and the word-as-picture. Sonnets are not included here because they require not only rhyme and meter, but a complex argument or narrative which must be worked out beforehand. A sonnet, for a child, is like a terribly long flight of stairs with no landings for relief. But a pantoum or villanelle, no matter how complex the form may initially appear, takes a few lines or words and uses them as counters to be moved around as sensibly as possible. Things do not proceed forward so much as back and forth, like a rondo, developing a music of its own. Extending from these, children can be encouraged to make up their own verse forms.

Poetic Forms

PANTOUM

A Malayan verse form consisting of quatrains in which the second and fourth lines are repeated as the first and third lines of the following quatrain, and in which the final line of the poem repeats the opening line. (See example.)

SESTINA

First choose six end words: make sure they are as interesting as possible since you will have to live with them for six stanzas. Then write lines to fit the end words.

These end-words recur throughout the six stanzas in a certain order: 123456, 615243, 364125, 532614, 451362, 246531. (The order is actually taking bottom end-word then top, bottom then top, bottom then top, from the preceding stanza.) Then follow with an *envoi* (a concluding stanza) of three lines. Each line contains two of the end-words—end-words 1 and 2 in the first line, 3 and 4 in the second, and 5 and 6 in the final line.

ODE

In praise of anything. Keep the focus on the particular subject, e.g., Ode to Television, Ode to My Feet, Ode to My Brains, Ode to Frankenstein, Ode to the Air.

HAIKU

The world's most overburdened form. However, it's worth trying, especially if you're teaching syllabification. In three lines, as close to 17 syllables as possible (5-7-5), set a quiet natural scene and then either shatter it or sum it up in the last line. Whole sentences need not be used. Most school haikus have an unreal preciousness. But you can freshen the observations by combining the writing with a nature trip—or dispensing with nature as a theme altogether.

Tanka: Same idea as haiku, except this time 31 syllables (5-7-5-7-7).

Cinquain: 2-4-6-8-2 syllables in a five-line poem.

PICTOGRAMS OR SHAPED POEMS

Building pictures with words. This idea has engaged serious poets from George Herbert's altar or wing-shaped poems to Ginsberg's Poem-Rocket or May Swenson's book of shaped poems, *Iconography* (Scribners), or Gregory Corso's *Bomb*. Words are arranged in line-lengths that actually make a picture in the process of speaking about the object.

LIMERICK

As everyone knows, this is a light or nonsensical verse of five lines with an aabba rhyme scheme. Suggest a place name or person's name in the first line; a limerick should be someone's story. Also fun to try to rhyme 2- and 3-syllable words.

CONCRETE POETRY

A popular, wide-open area in contemporary poetry, easier to recognize than to define. The point is to combine words, type and white space in an arrangement for pleasurable effect. It's a good way to see words and letters as objects in themselves; even white space becomes activated: the meeting of graphics and literature. The best way to introduce it is to bring in some books as examples: Mary Ellen Solt's *Concrete Poetry: A World-View*, Emmett Williams' *Anthology of Concrete Poetry*, Aram Saroyan's *Aram*, Norman Pritchard's *Matrix*.

ONE-WORD POEM

For better or worse I had come up with a new assignment: the one-word poem. It seemed simple enough for this class. I also thought it would be interesting to direct the children's attention to the fact that words are language, or, more to the point, that words are words, physical objects when written on a page. As opposed to the idea that words are only throw-away receptacles for ideas. That is, I wanted to give an assignment which would in itself suggest that even if you have a good idea you may not have a one-word poem, a poem consisting of one word only, and that they should pick their favorite word to write down. They didn't seem to understand, so I said further that they have a favorite color, right? Yeah, blue. OK. And a favorite month? Yeah, a favorite day? Yeah, Saturday! OK. How about your favorite word? I had given an example of a word: "dog." Then I explained that the word could be made up: "gsmlpgh." I also explained that it could be *like* a word they knew, but not necessarily the word itself: I gave as an example Aram Saroyan's immortal "lighght." I also said they could write as many one-word poems as they wished; or none at all. . . . A few children understood the assignment practically before I had finished explaining, and they were already hard at work. Most, however, sat in a sort of stunned silence, as if they were going insane. As I walked around the room, giving out correct spellings, these voices would ask me what they were supposed to do. It wasn't so much that they hadn't understood: I don't think they believed their ears. "Just *one* word?"

—Ron Padgett

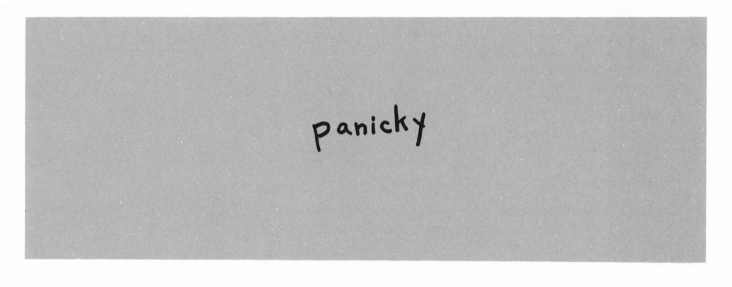

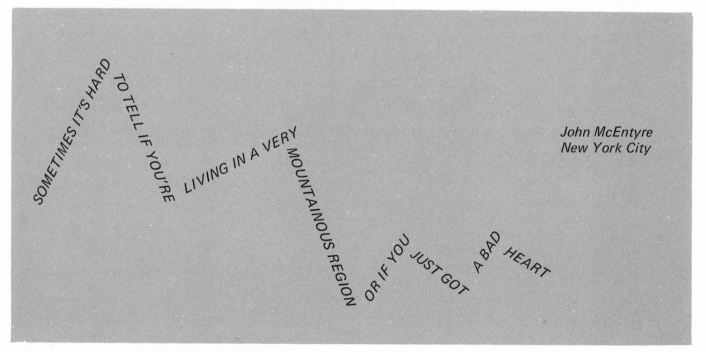

John McEntyre
New York City

I am writing Haiku.

People ran like cats,
Away from the thunder storm,
They fled for their lives.

Under the blue sky,
Over the beautiful stream
Stands a sturdy bridge.

Creatures of Darkness,
They glow like the big red sun,
Fireflies are they.

Birds fly to tree tops,
Grasshoppers hop to tall grass,
Nature has its way.

Galloping through woods,
Riding on the deep forests,
Killing all the men.

Today's just my luck,
I, the great king of all beast,
Catching all my prey.

Mon
4th Grade, P.S. 42
New York City

A blue Coat chases
me. I'm so scared I fly up
in the sky a bird.

Yuk
4th Grade
P.S. 42, N.Y.C.

(Cinquain)

The street
People hang out
In heat they wave and shout
They meet with knives that talk
about

The street.

Louis
Benjamin Franklin H.S.
New York City

TEARS ARE BROKEN EASILY (Pantoum)

And my tears go away
Dreaming of Santa Claus on Christmas Day crying
When it's Christmas Eve the tears stay
Snow is made out of ice and ice is made out of water

Dreaming of Santa Claus on Christmas Day crying
He falls asleep
Snow is made out of ice and ice is made out of water
And tears are made out of trying

He falls asleep
When his deer go drifting past
And tears are made out of trying
And I am made out of tears

When his deer go drifting past
And my tears go away
And I am made out of tears
When it's Christmas Eve the tears stay

Wendy van den Heuvel
New York City

Parallel poems are based on repetitions: they have consecutive lines that begin or end with the same words. This is a form that many poets have made use of (the composers of the Psalms, Whitman, Breton, etc.) often for its rhythmic chant-like effect. It's particularly easy for kids to do, and introduces them to the pleasure of literary form. The structure is there as something to be relied on, yet its open-endedness invites the writer to go further and further out in his imagination. The beauty of these parallel poem ideas is that they allow any student to plug into them at his own level of skill and sophistication. They also require a minimum of teaching explanation and lend themselves well to class collaborations and pairings—all of which may explain their recent popularity among teachers.

Parallel Poems and Lists

Some writer-teachers have grown disenchanted with this repetition approach, not because it doesn't work, but because one can go on forever in this vein, with the students hanging back to wait for the next formula to fill in as surely as they fill in the blanks in their notebooks. *Parallel poems are a good way to begin; they are only a limited answer.* Any of the ideas in this section can be sprung from the repetitive structure and used loosely as take-off points for other kinds of writing. Conversely, most writing ideas in other sections of this catalog can be streamlined into a parallel form, if that focus is desired. When working with a group, a teacher can turn almost anything kids are excited about discussing into a parallel poem; the question is, when will that form inhibit and when will it open the imagination?

Here is a representative sample of these ideas, developed during the four and one half years of the Teachers & Writers Collaborative, taken from the work of Kenneth Koch and from material compiled by a group of other poets—among them Ron Padgett, Dick Gallup, Larry Fagin, Phillip Lopate, Bill Zavatsky and David Shapiro—who have experimented extensively with these forms:

I wish

Write a poem in which every line begins with "I wish..."

Colors

Write a poem with a color in every line.

I Used to Be

Has the form "I used to be (a)_____ but now I'm (a) _____."

I Seem to Be

Has the form "I seem to be (a) _____ but I'm really (a) _____"

Lies

Write a poem with a lie in every line.
Write a poem with a whopping lie in every line.

I Remember

Write a poem in which every lines begins with "I remember....."

Dreams of the Future

Write a poem in which every line begins with "I am going to...."

Comparison poems

"_____ is like _____." E.g., Thunder is like bowling. Clouds are like a feather.

Equivalent poems

"In the past they _____ , but now we _____."

Descriptions

Metaphoric descriptions of classmates can occasionally be venomous, but there is plenty of opportunity here for kindness and wit. Here are some fourth-graders talking about their class:

Robert is like pretzels, a salty boy
Elaine is princess pretty
David is lemon, so sour
Teresa is a potato chip, she crackles
Diego upside down is all right
and Dominico is a backward rider
Karen has fish lips
        and John Store shoes
        on sale for ten cents
Maida is as loud as a mouse
Darlene is everything, everyday

You can also stimulate lively comparisons in this form:

If my mother were an animal she would be
(an intellectual prairie dog)
If my Laurie were music she'd be
(a slow sad song)
If my teacher were a taste he would be
(sharp and full of changes, like a pickle)

Metaphor poems

Same as Comparison poems, except without the "like."

Definitions

Spring is _____
Love is _____
War is _____
Fear is _____
etc.

THE THIRD EYE

The third eye can see the wolf eat the
        three little pigs
The third eye can't see the wolf fall
        in blazing fire
The third eye can't see me eat up the
        cooks
The third eye can't see me do homework
The third eye can see the world
The third eye can see the house with
        the red room.

Genett Way
P.S. 61, New York City

ONE DAY IN HIS LIFE

He is blue
He wakes up and pulls off his blue bedspread
He eats breakfast from a blue spoon and table
He goes out his blue door
He gets in his blue car
He goes to his blue office
He works at Pittsburg Paints and makes blue
He feels blue after his day at work
He goes to the Blue Room (a bar)
He gets home late his wife beats him black and blue

Peter Wilson
5th Grade
Twin Pines Day School
Oakland, California

Building a Monster
See example. After poem is finished perhaps have the children make drawings of the monster.

The Third Eye
Every line is about what the mysterious third eye (the mystical eye) sees that the other two don't.

In the Middle of the Night
Write a poem in which every line begins "In the middle of the night. . . ."

Going to Sleep
Write a poem describing how each thing in the universe goes to sleep.

Synaesthesia
What does a particular sound smell like? A certain color feel like? A texture sound like? Every line crosses two senses.

Catalogue Poem
A poem which has many different flowers (snap-dragon, marigold, daisy, sweet pea, begonia, anemones, phlox, forget-me-nots) for the sheer pleasure of the names if nothing else.

The Exploding Verb
Originally tried as "describe how things explode and what happens." E.g. "The teachers exploded when the kids were bad." "The sky exploded and it rained backwards."

But any dramatic or interesting verb could be substituted. (Try "dances," "boomerangs," "pees," "shines". . . .)

Lists
Make a list of 10 interesting things, for example:

10 things that could never happen
10 things I do every day
10 most beautiful girls in the world
10 things that go up/down

Inside/Outside
In a poem, tell what exists outside a thing and inside the same thing. E.g., "Outside the violin is air/inside is music waiting to be played." "Outside me is blue pants/inside me is red blood."

Combinations
Any of the above assignments can be combined to make them more challenging. For instance, putting a color and a lie in every line, or a wish and a noise.

MIXED LOVE

I love you as a drunk likes his beercan.
I love you because you are so beautiful but dumb
It makes me feel superior
I love the way you brush your hair like a witch
I love your dandruff, it makes you look like
White Christmas
I like the way you do the hippo walk
I love you like an old man loves a bikini
I love you like the moon likes the night
I love you like a hammer hits a nail
You and me are like hamburger and tomatoes
I love you as Nixon kisses Agnew
I love you like a kid loves Sesame Street
I love you like a cookie monster likes cookies
I love you like a peach, it tastes wundervar
Ah, ecstasy of it all!
I love the sun as I love myself
My name is Jamaica
I love you like the crust in my underwear
I love you like California loves Reagan
I love you like a pencil likes this writing paper.

Class 6-326
P.S. 75
New York City

ABOUT PEE

The sun pees in his bed
A horse pees out his tail
A duck pees by his mouth
A ghost pees out of his nose
A spaceman pees on top of his saucer
A hog pees from his ears and makes tears
A chair pees by his legs
Teeth pee by the point of a gumdrop
A toilet pees in a bowl
A man pees in his mouth
A man pees on top of the museum
A dog pees on top of the furniture
A cat pees on food—echk!
A cat pees on dog mess
A drawer pees where the flies live
A jacket pees by the zipper
A coat pees out its pocket
A devil pees by the fork and tail
A boat pees out the propeller
A garbage can pees on people's hands
A flower pees on the stems

Ronald and Ellen
Bedford-Lincoln MUSE
Brooklyn, New York

I REMEMBER

I remember having a dream about a pink elephant on a cloud
          saying "Welcome to dreamland".
I remember having a dream about my mother roasting our dog.
I remember over-turning the shopping cart.
I remember calling a peach a fuzzy apple.
I remember the dresses falling on me.
I remember making a hole in the ceiling with a super ball.
I remember knocking a hole in the bedroom wall with my feet.
I remember writing all over the new bedroom wall with crayons.
I remember watching my cousin throw mice on my mother.

                              Scott Lavender
                              Grade 6

TEN THINGS THAT COULD NEVER HAPPEN

1. A person could never have 9 faces.
2. Dinosaurs could never come back.
3. A person could not be the smartest.
4. Part funnybone, part funny man.
5. Cuckoo Cuckoo
6. Naked man walking in public
7. fried face
8. A sweater that was never used.
10. I, loving 8 boys.

                              CeCe
                              5th Grade
                              P.S. 75, New York City

I remember when I fell into a puddle of water.
I remember when I fell down my grandmother's stairs.
I remember when I spilled a whole cup of chlorine.
I remember when my cat died and I cried for 3 whole days.
I remember when my grandmother danced for one minute.
I remember when my little sister began to walk.
I remember when my dog went in our pool.
I remember explaining all strange things and my mother
          said I was the strangest thing.

                              Mary Grace Squitiere
                              Grade 6

DREAMS

The pencil dreams about writing the President a note.
The rubber band dreams of stretching and pulling itself apart.
The sun dreams of melting an ice cube.
The typewriter dreams of rough fingertips.
A door dreams of getting slammed.
A photographer dreams of taking pictures of children.
The camera dreams of taking pictures of the photographer.
The sidewalk dreams about being stepped on.
The hair dreams about getting cut.
The dream dreams about someone having him.
The dog dreams about getting a boat.
The dog dreams about taking a walk.
The cat dreams about having kittens.
A rabbit dreams about eating carrots.
The ant is dreaming about getting stepped on.
The house dreams about getting new shingles.
A star dreams about getting babies.
The balloon dreams about getting lost.
The baby dreams about growing up.
The man in the moon dreams of no astronauts on his moon.
A balloon dreams about getting popped.
Oh! What a horrible dream!
A person dreams about monsters and other monsters.
And Judy dreams about school and Arithmetic all day.
I'm dreaming of a special boy all bright, happy and gay.
I'm dreaming of no population.
I hope it happens soon.
I'm dreaming of a thousand dollars and how nice it would be.
The blackboard is dreaming of taking a trip and not teaching
       children anything, and is sick and tired of having to be
       written on and keeps spitting erasers, water, and
       chalk all over like crazy.

Class 3-17
Horace Mann School
Bayonne, New Jersey

IN THE MIDDLE OF THE NIGHT

The robot is stealing my mother.

John Cruikshank
1st Grade

WHAT IS THE COLOR OF LOVE

My love color is red Because
red is color of my blood.
And I love the color of blood
because my blood is red
And I love Blue because
the daylight is blue.
I love the color pink is
the color of the big big
tall circuses of United States
of America.
And Orange is best color
Because the biggest house
of them all are
Big that the big house,
EMPIRE STATE BUILDING. And
I love my hard red *love.*

Charles
4th Grade

BUILDING A MONSTER

The skull of a bald eagle
wig of a hippy
neck of a giraffe
head of a fly
nose of an anteater
back of a turtle
chest of a woman
legs of a centipede
arms of a spider monkey
tail of a pig
mouth of a porcupine
teeth of a wolf
bones of a kangaroo
fins of a salmon
laugh of a hyena
breath of an onion

Class 5-303
P.S. 75
New York City

I REMEMBER

I remember Florence breaking her nose,
I remember Jery's hairy hook shot,
I remember falling off the diving board,
I remember stupid dreams about being in school.
I remember singing the fourth side of Jesus Christ Superstar.
I remember I have two bucks in my pocket.
I remember fifth grade parties.
I remember my last two birthday parties.
I remember last week's poem.
I remember my one handed foul shot.
I remember that I haven't had one disease
I remember our President and vice president.
I remember sleeping in music.
I remember getting beer thrown at me.
I remember my leading role in the King and I and at tryouts
      I memorized the first two lines and when I was
      to say the 3rd I lost my place and I said, "Where
      are we." Everyone laughed.
I remember getting sick and throwing up on the 5th performance.

Ernest Michael Thomas Lettieri, Jr.
Grade 6

Materials

The materials listed on the following pages are supplemental to the assignments described elsewhere in The Whole Word Catalogue. The materials themselves are listed, with some gross separation of categories; and reference is made to assignments, which are capitalized.

Most materials are available in schools or through regular school suppliers. When not obtainable through these sources they can be found by scrounging around local stores. Most merchants discard enormous quantities of packing supplies that are very useful in the classroom.

An especially useful source list is the one published by Educational Development Center, 55 Chapel Street, Newton, Mass.

In addition to the supplemental aspect of this list, the materials themselves will suggest further possibilities to both the teacher and to the children. With unusual combinations of surfaces, implements, and equipment, new forms of writing and new writing activities will emerge. To encourage this sort of flexible use of materials, we include, at several points in this section, pages which simply list unusual combinations, with no reference to assignments.

Such a gaudy display of exciting materials is somewhat deceptive, however.

Often the more unusual ones will be used to seduce older, disenchanted children into writing; or to give young children who cannot yet manage handwriting easily a wide range of composing possibilities.

But the fact remains that writing, for those who are ready to focus on content and style, is most efficiently accomplished with paper that is of managable size, and a writing implement that does the job without distraction.

It is wrong to assume, however, that children of a certain age should be mature enough to do without the "gimmicks"; exciting materials suggest new possibilities at any age.

Surfaces

We have listed on the following pages a wide variety of writing surfaces. Such a variety, though not necessarily the same items, should be available in every classroom. Children will use almost any surface on which to write and draw, much to the dismay of many parents. This is a useful habit to encourage in the classroom, with due concern for practical matters. If a child wants to write on his desk, cover it with contac paper or a desk-size writing pad, taped down. If he wants to write on the wall, or the floor, cover them with less precious materials—cardboard or wrapping paper. Then the desk and walls are saved; so too is the child's eagerness to write.

VERY LARGE SURFACES

large sheets of newsprint
project roll paper (wrapping paper)
adding machine tape
sheets of cardboard
cardboard packing cases
huge cardboard tubes
chalkboard
walls
floors
boulders
glass (plate glass windows)
pre-fab wall pieces

* pre-fab wall pieces—building suppliers have large sheets of many substances.

* Adding machine tape can be found in office supply stores and is available in several widths.

* Sheets of cardboard—may be scrounged from trash. Large sheets of tri-wall (three ply) may be ordered from:

Tri-Wall Container Corp.
1 Dupont Street
Plainview, N.Y.

* Huge cardboard packing cases can be gotten from appliance stores that sell refrigerators, stoves, freezers, washing machines.

* Huge cardboard tubes can be found in carpet stores (a graffiti pillar?).

Large expanses of paper or other writing surfaces that are washable, disposable, or (sometimes) permanent, are ideal for unassigned, surreptitious writing.

Set aside a GRAFFITI WALL in your classroom where children know that they may write or draw anything they want, at any time. This may be a segment of the chalkboard, or more conveniently, huge sheets of cardboard or paper, propped or taped to a blank wall, or along the hall outside your room. Have an empty surface waiting for the time when the one in use is filled to capacity.

Children may write SECRETS on the inside surfaces of huge cardboard cartons ("caves") using a flashlight, or whatever natural light is available.

Sometimes find an unusual surface, such as a neighboring boulder (limestone is easiest, because it can be scratched), or a wall belonging to a friendly neighbor; to add a public dimension to your children's graffiti.

These surfaces are also good for COLLABORAT-IVE POEMS and STORIES, and DICTATED POEMS and stories, where it is helpful to keep the work, written large, in sight of the whole class.

CONTINUOUS POEMS and STORIES can be written along a strip of adding machine tape which is placed along the floor or wall (at child level) or kept wound around a conveniently placed dowel, or window-shade roller.

VERY SMALL SURFACES

SECRETS are best hidden on tiny pieces of paper.

The habit of passing notes should extend to the teacher who can send very important messages on little, personal bits of paper, and expect the same in return.

LETTERS may be posted in the class mailbox (made from cardboard box).

Ideas for writing activities may be contributed by children on file cards and kept in shoe boxes—ideas such as STRANGE SITUATIONS and WHAT IF's.

STANDARD SCHOOL PAPER SURFACES

school lined paper
manila—all sizes
newsprint—large sheets
"project" paper—wrapping paper, by the roll
construction paper—all sizes and colors
oaktag

Every assignment in this book could be done on paper that is regularly found in the classroom. Even here, the slightest variations can make great differences in the appeal of the assignment.

How About:
doing arithmetic on construction paper?
making scientific observations on project paper?
turning lined paper on its side and using the vertical columns for a chart of some sort?
sharing the oaktag with the children?

FRAME PAPER

TV script paper
homemade cartoon paper (large sheets of paper, ruled into four or more boxes)

* TV script paper is available in several sizes at arge office supply stores, and where commercial art materials are sold.

Commercial TV script paper or homemade cartoon paper may be used for writing comics, or any other story. The divisions help children isolate incidents and order action in an appropriate sequence.

TV script paper ("storyboard pad") looks like this:

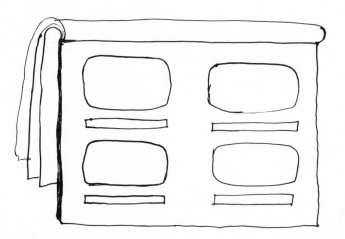

How About:

writing with colored chalk on the chalkboard?
writing with paints and paint rollers on any large surface?
arranging stones or bricks into words so that people in airplanes can read the message?
writing answers to spelling (and other tests) in finger paint or sand?
sewing letters into large pieces of fabric?
making large TV scripts by drawing and writing on a long strip of wrapping paper—to be shown on a cardboard box TV?
writing with a finger or arm in the air?
writing in water, sand, mud, dust?

How About:

outlawing pencils and pens sometimes (pretend you are living in a time before there were such things)—what else can messages be written with?
having a sentence with word cards always sitting along the chalk tray? Children can change one word, or many, as long as it continues to make sense (it can be silly sense, of course).
avoiding all handwriting situations for children who are especially fearful—have them type their spelling lessons, dictate their social studies, arrange their arithmetic problems and answers on their own private desk-sized flannel board (with symbols you and he have cut out together)?
making letters, words, sentences, by arranging straws, popsicle sticks, paper strips, twigs on surface—paste down or re-shuffle? Remember this is a novelty for older, proficient writers, but important for beginners.
making script letters and words with long pieces of yarn on horizontal flannel board, while children are still making manuscript letters?

How About:

pinning word cards on fabric wall hanging—making sentences, poems, stories, or simply messages?
making rubbings of sandpaper letters by first cutting large letters out of sandpaper, arranging them into words and pasting them to large surface, then rubbing clean paper (which has been placed over letters) with crayon or colored chalk?
making certain (after you have gotten to know this year's class) there is at least one printing device, or one set of paper or fabric letters, for every child who should not be forced to write by hand? This may require going to the hardware store and buying several alphabets' worth of rubber stamps.
slowing down and preparing some of your messages to the children in an inefficient, time-consuming way, like pasting letters or rubber stamping?

Printing

We are including in this section only those printing methods which can be employed with reasonable cost and satisfying results with children.

All of the equipment described here can be used by very young children, with the exception of the few methods which require cutting with sharp tools.

One general book with excellent detail on both hand and mechanical printing is *Step-By-Step Printmaking* by E. Schachner, Golden Press, Western Publishing Co.—paperback $2.

STAMPING

With fingers, hands, feet, heavy stock cut in shapes, linoleum blocks, wood blocks, vegetables cut in shapes, rubber stamps and pad.

A wonderful book on (or with) finger stamping is Ruth Krauss' *The Thumb-print*, 1967, Harper & Row.

ROLLING

Place any found or constructed inked shape between two clean pieces of paper, then roll with rolling pin or brayer.

There will be an imprint on both papers.

RUBBING

The word below is a rubbing and was made by:
1) cutting the letters from oak tag.
2) arranging them to make the word.
3) placing a clean paper over the letters, and
4) rubbing evenly with lead pencil (chalk, charcoal, crayon would have been as good).

MASKING

Place any found or constructed shapes on inked paper. Cover with clean paper and roll with rolling pin or brayer.

Remember: if you use cut out letters they must be reversed when arranged on the inked paper.

DUPLICATING

Every school has a duplicating machine of some sort, even if it has nothing else.

Mimeograph, rexograph and other such machinery are found invariably in inaccessible places like The Office.

Older children can make good use of this equipment. They can both cut the stencils and operate the machines.

Young children probably should not run the machines without close supervision because of the toxic inks required, but they can certainly make their own stencils.

And there is no more useful aide for the teacher. Everything the children write can be reproduced. Time to make the stencils is the only limiting factor, and there the teacher has lots of help.

LABEL MAKER

Commercial label makers are ingenious printing devices.

Educational Development Center (55 Chapel St. Newton, Mass.) has a fine booklet on printing with a label maker.

Try to buy the kind that will print letters in reverse, so that the final product will have the letters going the right direction. (It is possible to do it without this special kind; but harder.)

Also, try to get the widest tape possible for the biggest letters.

If you have a label maker that only prints letters going the "right" way:
1. make the strip on the label maker.
2. spread strip out, *letters down*—tape ends down, if necessary.
3. roll inked brayer over sticky back side of strip.
4. place clean paper over inked strip and roll with clean brayer.

If you have a label maker that reverses letters:
1. make the strip, but do each word, and each letter within each word *in reverse order*.
2. stick strip to some surface and ink raised letters.
3. place clean paper on inked letters and roll with brayer.

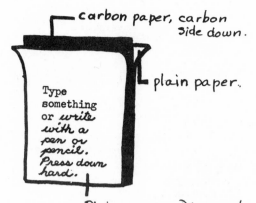

carbon paper, carbon side down.

plain paper.

Type something or *write with a pen or pencil. Press down hard.*

Plain paper. Discard after message has been written.

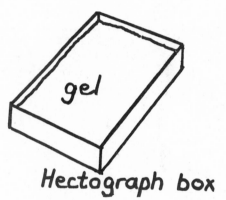

gel

Hectograph box

HECTOGRAPH

Hectograph printing is one of the cheapest and easiest classroom techniques for making multiple copies. A set may be purchased at stationery stores for under $5.00.

1. Arrange, from top to bottom, a plain piece of paper, a piece of carbon paper (brightly colored carbon paper is available) with carbon side down, and another plain piece of paper.
2. Write message on top sheet of plain paper using typewriter or sharp writing tool. Press down hard.
3. Press bottom paper on gel in hectograph box. Letters will transfer to gel. Letters will be reversed!
4. Press clean paper on gel. Letters will reverse again to proper direction on this final sheet. (You can make 25 copies or more.)
5. Wipe gel clean with damp sponge.

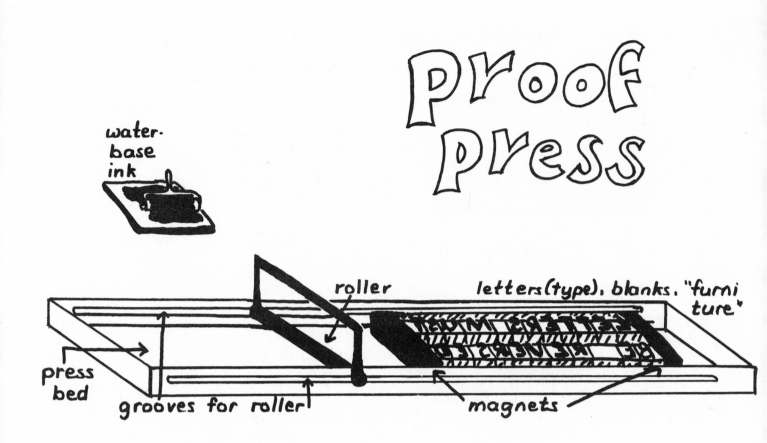

Proof Press

water-base ink

roller

letters (type), blanks, "furniture"

press bed

grooves for roller

magnets

PROOF PRESS

Proof presses can be purchased for reasonable prices at auctions or direct from print shops.

Recently we bought three proof presses ranging in price from $5.00 (at an auction in Vermont) to $25.00 (a "discard" from a print shop in New York City). Many print shops have old presses (and old wood type) that they no longer use.

Linoleum or woodcuts may be used as well as type.

1. Set type by arranging letters in reverse order, and then locking into place with heavy duty magnets. Many of the dime store four for 29¢ variety will do. Separate words with "blanks." Separate line from line with strips of card board or specially made "furniture."

2. Ink brayer by running brayer across a glass plate (or any other washable surface) until the brayer is evenly coated. Ink type by running inked brayer over letters.

3. Place paper over type. Pull press roller back and forth once.

BLUE PRINTING

Blue printing requires a little more space, supplies, and patience than many people can find.

But the results are both wonderful and startling.

The process, basically, is: specially treated paper (that used by architects in making blueprints!), when exposed to sunlight or a sunlamp, becomes fixed; but any area that is masked during exposure will be bleached white when the paper is dipped into a dilute hydrogen peroxide wash.

1. arrange objects to be printed on blueprint paper—can be:
   a body
   a found object
   cutout shapes or letters
   dark type on tracing paper

2. expose to direct sunlight or to sunlamp—experiment with time. Lamp will take longer—blue should be bleached to a very pale color.

3. dip in a very dilute peroxide bath until "negative" areas are bleached white—exposed areas will turn cobalt blue.

DISPLAY OF MATERIALS

A wide variety of writing assignments and materials may pass unnoticed and unused in a classroom if they are not displayed in a highly visible and appealing manner.

Even more than the attractiveness of such displays (and decoration is very much a matter of personal taste and inclination), there is an underlying assumption here that all materials are to be completely accessible to the children if they are to be used to full advantage.

DISPLAY OF WORKING MATERIALS

Make a child-height mobile or "tree" by hanging large plastic containers (with the tops cut off) from the ceiling or by tying them to a standing pipe or pole.

Arrange brightly decorated coffee tins on shelves.

Use the plastic containers or the decorated tins to display:

writing implements, scissors, straight edges, squeeze bottles containing paint, brushes, adhesives (school glue and paste, rub'n' glues, sprays—for teachers and older children) printing supplies (inks, brayers, cleaning materials), paper clips.

Provide secluded working surface for:

typewriter,

papers, and

writing tools.

Place printing equipment on a large, child-height working surface.

Decorate large boxes with separators and place on backs or stand on sides for: all kinds of paper cardboard sheets

Decorate the boxes you can get in liquor stores (the kind with square separators) for tubes of:

Contac paper, mylar, cardboard (the ones that come inside paper towels, toilet tissues, etc.), aluminum foil, paper towels. Dowels, horizontal and strong, within reach of children, may be used to hold: Roll of "project paper," roll of blueprint paper (keep covered until ready to use), masking tape (several sizes), mystic tape (many colors), adding machine tape, balls of yarn and thread.

Decorated cardboard or metal bins for magazines, fabric, scraps of paper.

Decorate a liquor store box and place in separate sections the following puppet-making supplies:

paper bags, paper scraps, other scraps, old newspaper (for rolling or cutting into papier mache), balloons, sticks or dowels, string and yarn, non-toxic papier mache glaze, water base paints.

**Books
and
Other
Resources**

For some time, we have been trying to convince publishers that students enjoy reading the work of other students. They often find it more engaging than the machine-turned prose and poetry of adult writers who "specialize" in writing for children. Now the number of anthologies of children's (and young people's) writing has sky-rocketed in the past few years, to the point where it's virtually impossible to keep track of all of them. So please forgive the omissions.

Yet many of the books are not what we bargained for. Rather than serving as vehicles through which young people can talk to each other, they are coffee-table books for adults who are interested in finding out what kids are thinking about these days and whether they're as cute as they used to be on Art Linkletter's show. In any case here is a rundown, in no particular order, of collections of writing by young people, many of which will speak to the interests and feelings of any number of student readers.

Marvin Hoffman

ANTHOLOGIES

The Voice of the Children Ed. by Terri Bush and June Jordan. Holt, Rinehart & Winston, 1970. $1.95 paper.

This is a collection of poems by Black and Puerto Rican junior high school students who have been writing together for almost four years. (Sad to say, they have disbanded this past year.) Out of regular Saturday sessions in local churches and community centers and summers together in the country they have produced a weekly magazine of student writing, from which selections were made for this book.

I must admit to a special bias in favor of this book. VOC was begun under Teachers & Writers Collaborative, and although it has long since become independent, we know the kids and the directors and we have watched them grow together and fight together.

Although there are a number of fine pieces in the anthology, I remember a number from their weekly paper which I liked better than some that have been included here. Nonetheless this is a book that *was* written for other students to read.

Miracles (1966), *Journeys* (1969), *There Are Two Lives* (1970) All edited by Richard Lewis and published by Simon & Schuster. *Miracles* $6.95, others $4.95.

None of these three collections by Richard Lewis is available in paperback. This makes them a bit extravagant for classroom use which is a shame since they include some extraordinarily beautiful work by children from all over the world. *Miracles* is an international collection of poetry; *Journeys*, an international collection of prose; and *There Are Two Lives*, a collection of translated poems by Japanese schoolchildren.

To my mind the two poetry collections are more successful. The work of the Japanese children is absolutely extraordinary—personal and uninhibited in a way I hardly expected from what little I know of the tightness and formality of Japanese society. I

once wrote out several poems from this book in the form of letters to students in a class I was working with and had the children write responses to them.

All three books are certainly worth a look.

The Me Nobody Knows Ed. by Steven Joseph, 1969, Avon Paperback, 95¢.

This may be one of the most famous student anthologies ever published, partly because it served as the source for a highly successful Broadway musical show of the same name. It too is a collection of prose and poetry from ghetto children in New York. Although it contains some powerful writing I find it somewhat exploitative of the pathological aspects of ghetto living—drugs, rats, garbage, etc. These are valid subjects for students to deal with in their writing, subjects whose existence is often shamefully denied in schools. But it's not *all* there is to any child's life.

Can't You Hear Me Talking To You Ed. by Caroline Mirthes, Bantam Original paperback. Out of print.

A more recent collection than *The Me Nobody Knows*. Unlike the Joseph anthology these pieces were all done by children in one school on the Lower East Side of New York and compiled by their teacher. All the pieces are prose compositions, undoubtedly written in response to class or homework assignments. The writings are intensely powerful. One section entitled "Who Am I" I gave to a group of 5th graders to read and they responded with some of their own best work. The book's major weakness is the personal introduction by the editor to the works of each student which makes the whole collection seem too much like a sociological case study. The students' work is good enough to stand by itself.

Talking About Us Ed. by Bill Wertheim. 1970, New Century paperback $3.50; distributed by Hawthorn Books.

For some unaccountable reason there are almost no good collections of writing by high school students. *Talkin' About Us* is one of the rare exceptions. The work was collected from students in Upward Bound programs all over the country and includes poetry and prose by Black, Puerto Rican, Chicano, Indian Eskimo, and Appalachian White youngsters. There are places where the writing approaches professional quality and all of it would make engaging reading for any high school student.

How Old Will You Be In 1984 Ed. Diane Divoky. Avon paperback, $1.25.

Our Time Is Now by John Birmingham. Praeger, hardcover, 1970, $5.95. Out of print.

These books are basically collections of writings from the high school underground press. The Birmingham book also contains a long first-person account by the author of his own experiences in setting up an underground paper. The writings are sometimes humorous, often polemical, and extremely difficult to read in large doses. This is also the kind of writing that becomes dated very quickly (much of this work comes from 1967-69). Nonetheless it is a more accurate representation of what's on the minds of many high school students than the essays they produce for their English courses.

Letter To A Teacher From The Schoolboys of Barbiana with postscripts by Robert Coles and John Holt. Vintage Paperback, $1.95.

This is an extraordinary book. It was written by a group of working-class students in a small Italian town who had been students in a special school established by a village priest. It is not a literary anthology, but an attempt to describe from the students' point of view the shortcomings of their public schools—teaching methods, teacher attitudes, class conflicts, and a number of other issues. It is written in a lucid and powerful style which is ideally suited to carrying their unusual message. Their comments on the teaching of writing (Pp. 14-15 and 118-19) are especially worth reading.

Here is a list of other anthologies; some of them we've heard about but never seen; others we've looked at and don't have too much to comment on, other than to let you know they exist.

Here I Am: An Anthology of Poems Written By Young People in Some of America's Minority Groups Ed. by Virginia Olsen Barron. Dutton Co., hardcover $5.95.

I Heard A Scream In the Streets Ed. by Nancy Larrick. M. Evans Company, New York, 1970. 95¢.

Children of Longing Ed. by Rosa Guy. Bantam Paperback Original, 1970. Out of print.

Chicory: Young Voices from the Black Ghetto Ed. by Sam Cornish and Lucian W. Dixon. Association Press, 1969. Hardcover out of print; paper $1.75.

The Excitement of Writing Ed. by A.B. Clegg. Chatto and Windus, 1969, London.

Let The Children Write: An Explanation of Intensive Writing Margaret Langdon. Longmans, Green and Co., London, 1961.

"Writing" Special issue of *English In Education*, Vol. 3, # 3, Autumn 1969, Journal of National Association for the Teaching of English. 5 Imperial Road. Huddersfield, Yorkshire, England.

Mother, These Are My Friends Ed. Mary Anne Gross. Published by City Schools Curriculum Service, 60 Commercial Wharf, Boston, Mass. (These are short pieces by young children with space for illustrations by the reader.)

RESOURCE BOOKS

What we have here are books with ideas about teaching writing, books describing personal experiences in the teaching of writing, and specific how-to books with detailed information on printing, codes, etc. Again, the list is not exhaustive. Additional books are mentioned in the MATERIALS and ASSIGNMENTS sections of this catalogue.

Wishes, Lies and Dreams by Kenneth Koch. Hardcover, Chelsea House, $7.95. Vintage paperback, $2.45.

There were books about children's writing before this one and there will be many others to follow, but none has received so much attention and none has impelled so many people—teachers and writers—to break with traditional approaches to classroom writing. In this book, Mr. Koch describes his own writing experiments with classes at P.S. 61 in Manhattan. He shows what beautiful poems children are capable of writing when they are freed of the traditional constraints of rhymed lines and "proper" sentiments. Mr. Koch replaced rhyming with repetitive structures of a formula nature (start each line with "I wish. . .," include a color in each line, use a noise in each line, etc.). At the same time he encouraged the students to be as "crazy" as they chose (to see green monkeys or to contend that one had once been a fish). Half the book is taken up by examples of the extraordinary work his students produced.

Yet there are problems. The formula quality of many of the assignments is one that encourages mindless mimicking by less inspired practitioners. Moreover, as we suggest in several other places in the catalogue, formulas and gimmicks are fine openers but they can be a terrible dead end if one fails to move beyond them into more sustained, more independently initiated writing.

Reservations aside, Mr. Koch's book is the best possible introduction to children's writing for the uninitiated.

Writers As Teachers: Teachers As Writers Ed. Jonathan Baumbach. Holt Rinehart & Winston, 1970. Hardcover $5.95. Paper $2.45.

This is a fine collection of essays by professional writers, consisting largely of accounts of their own attempts to teach writing. Just about all the material is based on teaching experiences at the college level, but this does not limit its usefulness to people working, say, at the high school level. There are many useful and useable ideas about writing approaches in sections like John Hawkes' account of the Voice Project at Stanford University and, in general, a lot of healthy, thoughtful self-criticism by writer-teachers like Denise Levertov, Wendell Berry and others.

36 Children by Herbert Kohl. New American Library (World Publishing Co.) 1967. Paperback 95¢.

This is another "early" classic (in this time when generations are measured in two-year cycles.) It is a description of Herb Kohl's teaching experiences in a Harlem school. It was a class in which writing played a central role—fables, myths, autobiographies—all of them generously sampled in the book, but surrounded by Herb's sensitive observations about schools, children, bureaucracies, and himself. We have a particular soft spot for this book since it led indirectly to the creation of Teachers & Writers Collaborative, of which Herb served as the first director.

A Student-Centered Language Arts Curriculum, Grades K-12: A Handbook for Teachers James Moffett. Houghton Mifflin Co., 1970. ($11.50)

I know a number of teachers whom I respect who are using this book as a resource for their own "language arts" programs. I must confess to having been unable to plow my way through its considerable number of pages. It is an extremely ambitious attempt to lay out a sequential curriculum for writing, language, and expression, from kindergarten through high school. Its major strength is that is activity-oriented; any reader will be rewarded with a number of interesting ideas for use in their own classes—theater games, writing assignments, etc. I find the emphasis on sequential development just doesn't match what I've seen of the idiosyncracies of individual children's styles and rhythms of development. It encourages a kind of simplistic thinking and a new orthodoxy which I doubt that Moffett favors.

In the Early World by Elwyn Richardson. 1964, Pantheon Books $7.95 Paper $4.95.

This is one of the most beautiful books, both in appearance and content, that I have ever read. For years it was an underground classic which was available only from the New Zealand Council for Educational Research (Mr. Richardson is a New Zealander). But two years ago Pantheon reprinted the book, and for that service is deserving of a medal. The text of the book consists of Mr. Richardson's sometimes difficult-to-follow account of his work with Maori children in a rural New Zealand school.

But more impressive than Mr. Richardson's own words are the countless examples of exquisite poetry, linoleum cuts, ceramics which his children produced. He is clearly a gifted teacher but I certainly wish I knew more about how he did it.

What Do I Do Monday? by John Holt. E.P. Dutton & Co, 1970. $8.95.

In this book John Holt attempts to lay out some practical suggestions for more imaginative approaches to classroom activities. Presumably there are enough people around now who are weary of criticizing and being criticized and who are eager to get down to concrete ideas about change.

Holt devotes a chapter in the book to writing and language in which he lays out a number of useful activity ideas. Some of his material is based on Moffett's book, but it is presented more loosely and more appealingly here.

Children Write Poetry: A Creative Approach by Flora Arnstein. Dover paperback, 1967, $2.50.

This is a genuine old classic, written several decades ago, well before the recent wave of interest in children's writing. Mrs. Arnstein describes her work in a private school in San Francisco where she taught her children to write poetry. She championed the then unpopular notion that rhyme and other poetic conventions constricted the expression of real emotion in original language. Her book contains a number of examples of the disastrous effects of adherence to poetic conventions as well as positive examples of the fruits of liberation from the constraints. Perhaps a bit dated, but still worth reading.

Children Printing; Printing With Labels Published by the Elementary Science Study, of Education Development Center, 55 Chapel Street, Newton, Mass.

Like a number of other ESS pamphlets (*Shadows, Batteries,* and *Bulbs*), these two are extremely simple, straightforward accounts of the ingenious printing work which can be done with very simple equipment in the classroom. The materials and ideas are eye-openers and you can take it from there.

Step-By-Step Printmaking By E. Schachner. Golden Press, Western Publishing Co., paperback $2.95.

An excellent primer on the varieties of printing techniques. It will help familiarize you with the terminology and equipment of printing and make it easier to cope with the more complicated sources you might wish to consult. A very attractively illustrated book.

The Lore and Language of Schoolchildren by Iona and Peter Opie, Oxford Univ. Press, hardcover $12.50, paper $5.50.

A magnificent compilation of children's games, chants, rhymes, superstitions; largely, though not exclusively, gathered from British sources. This does not limit its usefulness for American readers. It will put you back in touch with forgotten details of your own childhood culture and street play.

Children's Writing: A Sampler for Student Teachers by David Holbrook, Cambridge Univ. Press, New York, 1967, $2.75.

An interesting British work on children's writing. Very specific, many examples. A bit too heavy on psychoanalytic interpretation.

Making It Strange Vols. I-VII, and a manual. Published by Synectics Education System. Distributed by Harper & Row, New York. Each Volume, $2.20.

Accounts by people who have used the material continue to intrigue me. As far as I can gather it is an approach to the encouragement of metaphoric thinking which was developed in—of all places—industrial management, problem-solving programs.

I Know A Place by Robert Tannen. City Schools Curriculum Service, 60 Commercial Wharf, Boston, Mass.

A modest, inoffensive workbook in several volumes which lays out a structure to guide a student through the writing of his own story.

Improvisations for the Theatre: A Handbook of Teaching and Directing Techniques. By Viola Spolin, Northwestern Univ. Press, 1963. Text edition $6.95.

Theater is not my strong point, but a number of actors, directors and teachers have told me that this book is an unmatched source of theater games and improvisational techniques which are directly usable in the classroom.

How to Write Codes & Send Secret Messages by John Peterson. Scholastic Books, 60¢.

There are a number of books like this one which I've seen in school libraries and elsewhere. There's nothing more exciting to elementary school kids than secrecy, excluding and including others in their group, etc. This can be capitalized on to create some interesting games and exercises which have a good deal to teach, implicitly, about the structure of language.

Absolutely Mad Inventions Ed. by A.E. Brown and H.A. Jeffcott, Jr. Dover Paperback $1.50.

The editors have gone through the files of the U.S. Patent Office and have put together a collection of the craziest inventions patented—dimple tools, vermin electrocutors, safety coffins. I have brought it to my classes many times; it's hard to resist writing up your own pet projects. Let me tell you about my catalogue exterminator. . . .

There are a growing number of inexpensive collections of song lyrics—pop, rock, soul, blues—which some of our writers have used to inspire writing by students who love music but "hate" poetry. I must admit that this is not a genre that I feel comfortable with or happy about. Most of the song-inspired poetry I've seen by junior high and high school kids seems to underscore what's worst about the writing of that age—cliche, banality, false romanticism. In any case here are two collections and if you like them you can track down all the Beatles, Rolling Stones, Dylan songbooks that abound.

The Poetry of the Blues Samuel Charters, Avon Paperback, $1.25.

The Poetry of Rock by Richard Goldstein. Bantam Original Paperback $1.25.

MAGAZINES AND MISCELLANEOUS PUBLICATIONS

Foxfire Published quarterly by Southern Highlands Literary Fund, Rabun Gap, Georgia 30568. Subscriptions $5.00/year.

This is one of the most extraordinary publications I have ever come across, my dream of what every high school student could be doing. For the past five years a group of high school students in this small Appalachian town, under the supervision of Eliot Wigginton, one of their teachers, have been recording and paying homage to the rapidly disappearing culture and skills of their community. The magazine consists of material gathered from interviews with old people in the area on such subjects as chair caning, hog butchering, chimney building, ghost stories, home remedies, courtship. It's an inspired kind of anthropology, done from within the culture itself, not in order to bring to light some quaint local customs but to put one generation back in touch with its roots through a respectful encounter with their elders.

It's beautifully written, beautifully put together—altogether an inspired idea. If you can't get hold of the magazine, Doubleday has published a two volume collection of the best articles.

The Paper Inc. Mark duPree, c/o Justice, 612 Sharp Building, Lincoln, Nebraska 68508.

Something exciting to put up on the classroom wall—a kind of oversized broadsheet containing a few good poems at a time, written by lower-graders and beautifully handset and printed by their teachers.

Big Rock Candy Mountain 1115 Merril St., Menlo Park, Cal. 94025. Pub'd. quarterly. No longer being published. Back copies available.

This publication is from the same people who bring you the *Whole Earth Catalog*. It is an extremely valuable compendium of educational materials for teachers who are interested in experimenting with new approaches and new philosophies in their classrooms. Like its parent publication, the catalogue triggers off endless associations and ideas as you read each page, which is just what a catalogue is for—to be used as a stimulant, not as a tranquilizer.

In Feburary of 1971 BRCM did an entire issue on children's writing which we recommend highly, but any issue is a valuable resource for teachers and parents.

BLACK LIST: THE CONCISE REFERENCE GUIDE TO PUBLICATIONS AND BROADCASTING MEDIA OF AFRO-AMERICA, AFRICA AND THE CARIBBEAN.

291 pages. Colleges, book clubs, publishers, bookstores, advertising, public relations and literary agents, newspapers, periodicals and broadcasting stations operated for, by or about Blacks. Internat'l sections include info. on embassies, U.N. missions and other internat'l orgs. $12.50; fall 1972 supplement $8.50. Write "Black List", Panther House Ltd., Box 3552, New York, N.Y. 10017.

GRANTS AND AWARDS

A complete listing of those available to American writers; updated annually; believed to be only one giving information on both domestic and foreign grants. Write to "Listing of Grants and Awards Available," P.E.N. American Center, 156 Fifth Ave., N.Y., N.Y. 10010. Enclose $2.00 for non-members; $1.00 for P.E.N. members.

State Arts Councils

Many have poetry projects, including poetry-in-the-schools. For information, write your own state arts council. For complete list of state arts councils, send $2.00 to Associated Councils of the Arts, 1564 Broadway, New York, N.Y. 10036. Phone (212) 586-3731.

Community Arts Councils

Some are interested in poetry programs; complete list of community arts councils in each state is available for $1.00 from Associated Councils of the Arts (address above).

Resources for the Teaching of English (catalogue) for free copy write: National Council of Teachers of English, 1111 Kenyon Road, Urbana, III. 61801

A Useful List Of Classroom Items That Can Be Scrounged Or Purchased. from: Early Childhood Education Study, Educational Development Center, 55 Chapel Street, Newton, Mass. 02160

Supplies for the School Print Shop (Catalogue #70) Globe Printers Supply Co. 407 Mulberry Street, Newark, New Jersey

The prices here are a little high, but for anyone interested in printing in the classroom, this will at least give you a sense of the available materials which are manufactured commercially.

Directory of Little Magazines, Small Presses, Underground Newspapers 1970. Published by Dustbooks, Len Fulton, Publisher, 5218 Scottwood Rcad, Paradise, Calif. 95969. $2.50.

Contributors' Notes

ART BERGER is a poet whose work has appeared in several major anthologies and on two albums, *Poems for Peace* and *New Jazz Poets*. He is the author of *Blow the Man Down*, a book of poems.

ROSELLEN BROWN's book of poetry, *Some Deaths in the Delta* (U. of Mass. Press), was a National Arts Council Selection in 1970. A collection of her short stories, *Street Games*, was published by Doubleday in 1974.

MERLE MOLOFSKY CHIANESE is a novelist and playwright, born in New York in 1942. A chapter from *Street*, her novel in progress, is scheduled for publication in *Storefront*—an anthology of new American writing. She has completed the MFA program at Columbia and teaches at Medgar Evers college in Brooklyn.

BOB CLAWSON is an educational publisher at CSCS in Boston. CSCS produces participation textbooks, books which students have an opportunity to co-author.

LILA EBERMAN was one of the teachers at Benjamin Franklin H.S. who helped create material for the preliminary Fables unit.

LARRY FAGIN is the author of a booklet of poems called *Brain Damage*.

NORM FRUCHTER is director and part of the core staff of Independence H.S., an alternative school for dropouts in the Ironbound section of Newark. He is the author of the novels *Coat Upon A Stick* and *Single File*, and has made several films, including *Troublemakers—Community Organizing in Newark*, and *People's War* (filmed in North Vietnam).

DICK GALLUP was born in 1940 in Greenfield, Mass., and attended Tulane and Columbia. He has worked with young poets at MUSE in Brooklyn and he teaches a poetry workshop at the St. Marks Poetry Project in Manhattan. Mr. Gallup's first collection of poetry, *Where I Hang My Hat*, was published by Harper & Row.

HANNAH GREEN is the author of the novel *Dead of the House* (Doubleday), a best seller in 1972. She is associate professor of writing at the Columbia School of the Arts.

DAVID HENDERSON was born in Harlem in 1942. His poetry and writings have appeared in *Poems Now; The East Village Other; New Negro Poets, USA!*; and *Where Is Vietnam*. He has published a volume of his own poetry, *Felix of the Silent Forest* (1967).

MARVIN HOFFMAN, former director of TWC, has published articles in *The New Republic* and *The Nation*. He now supervises teacher training at Antioch College, New Hampshire.

LEN JENKINS, a novelist, is co-director of Total Effect, an educational consultants organization.

MARC KAMINSKY is the author of two books of poetry, *Birthday Poems* (Horizon Press) and *A New House* (Inwood/Horizon Press), and a book about poetry groups with old people, *What's Inside You It Shines Out of You* (Horizon Press).

KAREN KENNERLY was formerly Research Assistant at TWC. She was co-author of the preliminary Fables unit with Herb Kohl.

HERB KOHL is the author of *36 Children, The Open Classroom, Teaching the Unteachable* and *Math and Writing Games in the Open Classroom*.

MARTIN KUSHNER was director of TWC. He studied acting and directing at Yale Drama School, produced street theater in New York and Boston, and directed at Smith College and the U. of Pittsburgh.

DOUGHTRY LONG was born in Atlanta, Ga., and attended W. Va. State College. He has an MFA from Columbia School of the Arts in 1971.

PHILLIP LOPATE is the author of a volume of poems, *The Eyes Don't Always Want to Stay Open* (Northhampton Press) and a novella, *In Coyoacan* (Swollen Magpie Press). His works have appeared in the anthologies *A Cinch, Equal Time*, and other magazines. He is coordinator of TWC's special program at P.S. 75 in New York City and has written a book about his work there, *Being With Children* (Doubleday).

CLARENCE MAJOR was born in Atlanta, Ga. in 1936. His recent publications include *All-Night Visitors*, a novel (Olympia Press); *A Dictionary of Afro-American Slang* (International Publishers); and

Swallow the Lake, poetry (Wesleyan Univ. Press). He is the editor of *The New Black Poetry* (International Press, 1969). Mr. Major's work includes a novel, *NO* (Emerson Hall Pub's); poems, *Private Line* (Paul Bremman, Ltd., London); and poems, *Symptons In Madness* (Corinth).

RICHARD MURPHY, former associate director of TWC, is helping to run teacher workshops in Vermont.

SHEILA MURPHY, former School Coordinator for TWC, teaches a kindergarten class at Fairley (Vt.) Elementary School.

CRISTY NOYES is a student in the MFA program at Columbia School of the Arts. She worked at P.S. 75 (NYC) in the fall of 1971.

RON PADGETT was born in Tulsa, Ok. in 1942. He has published *Bean Spasms* with Ted Berrigan, and co-edited the *Anthology of New York Poets* with David Shapiro. He is the author of *Great Balls of Fire* (1969, Holt, Rinehart) and *The Adventures of Mr. and Mrs. Jim and Ron* (1970, Grossman), illus. by Jim Dine.

LENNOX RAPHAEL was born in 1940 in Trinidad. Before coming to the U.S. he worked as a reporter in Jamaica. His work has appeared in *American Dialog, Negro Digest*, and Clarence Major's anthology, *The New Black Poetry*. He has been a staff writer for *The East Village Other*. His play *Che* was produced off Broadway.

ANNE SEXTON wrote *Live or Die*, which won the Pulitzer Prize in 1967.

BILL ZAVATSKY edits two poetry magazines, *Sun* and *Roy Rogers*. His poetry has appeared in a number of magazines including *The World* and *Juillard*.

THE WHOLE WORD CATALOGUE (72 pages) is a practical collection of assignments for stimulating student writing, designed for both elementary and secondary students. Activities designed as catalysts for classroom exercises include: personal writing, collective novels, diagram stories, fables, spoof and parodies, and language games. It also contains an annotated bibliography.

A DAY DREAM I HAD AT NIGHT (119 pages) is a collection of oral literature from children who were not learning to read well or write competently or feel any real sense of satisfaction in school. The author, Roger Landrum, working in collaboration with two elementary school teachers, made class readers out of the children's own work, recorded the readers in a tape library, and designed a set of language exercises based on the readers.

IMAGINARY WORLDS (110 pages) was derived from an attempt to find themes of sufficient breadth and interest to allow sustained independent writing by students. Children invented their own Utopias, their own religions, new ways of fighting wars, different schools. They produced a great deal of extraordinary writing, reprinted in this book.

TEACHERS & WRITERS COLLABORATIVE NEWSLETTER, issued three times a year, draws together the experience and ideas of the writers and other artists who conduct T&W workshops in schools and community groups. A typical issue contains excerpts from the detailed work diaries and articl the artists, along with the works of the studen outside contributions.

SPRING 1973 NEWSLETTER (159 pages) ordered as a separate book. Of unusual interest issue are two articles, one by Anne Martin teaching of writing to first graders, the ot Phillip Lopate on making videotapes with el school children (from writing and producing through to editing and screening).

POSTER cover of the Fall 1973 issue Newsletter. Full size (17 by 22).

FIVE TALES OF ADVENTURE (119 page collection of short novels written by cl Teachers & Writers has published them for a audience of children as literature and as a text. The stories cover a wide range of styl interests—a family mystery, an urban sa Himalayan adventure, a sci-fi spoof, and a murder and retribution.